Sandy Creek
NEW YORK

An Imprint of Sterling Publishing
387 Park Avenue South
New York, NY 10016

ISBN 978-1-4351-5016-4

Manufactured in Heng Gang Town, China
Lot #:
2 4 6 8 10 9 7 5 3 1
06/13

SPIES
AND SPYING

Clive Gifford

Top Secret

Sandy Creek
NEW YORK

TABLE OF CONTENTS

WHAT IS SPYING?

SPYING, OR ESPIONAGE, INVOLVES THE UNCOVERING AND COLLECTION OF IMPORTANT INFORMATION, WHICH IS KNOWN AS INTELLIGENCE.

Intelligence comes in many forms, from learning what a nation plans to do with its economy to obtaining plans of a new aircraft or military weapon. It is gathered in dozens of different ways, from satellites and electronic systems tracking military forces to individual spies deep inside a country's government stealing political secrets. All countries spy on enemy nations, groups, and individuals considered a threat in some way to their security. Even seemingly friendly nations may spy behind each others' backs as each country seeks to gain an advantage.

Spying may seem glamorous in books and movies, but in the real world it can be grim and highly illegal. Real spies have carried out acts of sabotage, "black bag jobs" (break-ins) and assassinations – murders of people considered to be a threat.

LOOK CLOSER

During World War II, British saboteurs put dead rats filled with explosives in German coal stores. When the rats were shoveled into a train's furnace, the locomotive would explode.

◄ *Countries often use spies to protect their own secrets by investigating threats and rooting out enemy spies at work. This is called counter-intelligence.*

▼ *Two security officials watch a massive bank of close circuit television (CCTV) cameras. This is a form of surveillance – the close monitoring of the activities of a person or group. Surveillance is a crucial spying activity.*

INTELLIGENCE AGENCIES

Intelligence agencies are the organizations responsible for most spying. Famous among them are the Russian SVR (which is the agency that developed from a branch of the KGB), the French DGSE, Israel's Mossad, and the CIA of the United States. Many countries split their spying into home and abroad. In Britain, for example, MI5 deals largely with spying at home, while the Secret Intelligence Service, also known as MI6, is responsible for much of the spying overseas.

In 1985, the French DGSE tried to bomb, secretly, a ship owned by Greenpeace.

The *Rainbow Warrior* was sunk but the agents were captured, causing a major scandal.

TYPES OF SPY

THERE ARE MANY DIFFERENT TYPES OF SPY. SOME HOLD OFFICE JOBS WHERE THEY ARE EXPERTS IN LANGUAGES, CODES, COMPUTING, WEAPONRY, OR A COUNTRY OR REGION. OTHERS ORGANIZE MISSIONS OR KEEP TARGETS UNDER SURVEILLANCE. ONLY A SMALL NUMBER SPY IN OTHER COUNTRIES.

People become spies out of a sense of loyalty to their own country, for money, or, in some cases, because they are forced to do so by blackmail or threats. Some of the spies who are most valuable to their spymasters are those who have been recruited from a rival nation. These people may be defectors who have fled their own country and tell all in return for a guarantee of safety. Alternatively, they may be moles who appear to be working for one nation's military or spying agencies, but in actuality are spying for another country.

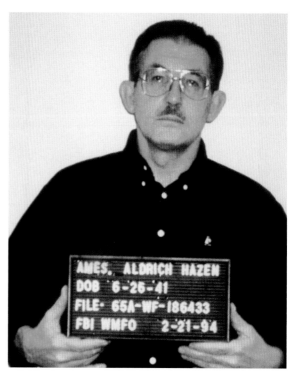

▲ Aldrich Ames was a mole inside the CIA. He was paid by the KGB to supply details of CIA missions and agents in the Soviet Union and elsewhere.

SPY EQUIPMENT

Money and resources are put into equipping modern spies with the tools that they need. Bugs are small electronic devices that are used to record or broadcast what is being said to a receiver nearby. These devices have been hidden in hotel rooms, meeting-places, and even in hollowed out rocks, tree stumps, and fake animal droppings! Taps are similar devices that can be fitted to phones so that an agent can listen in on calls.

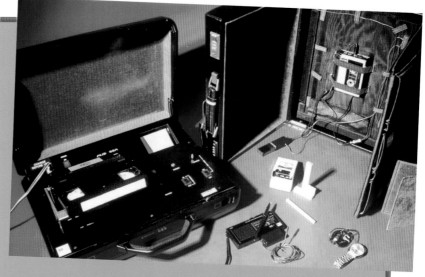

▲ Many spy gadgets are now available to the public. This collection includes a briefcase with a hidden video camera and sound recorders fitted inside cigarette packets and watches.

ANTONIO MENDEZ

Antonio Mendez was an artist and technical illustrator who became a CIA expert in disguise. During his 25-year career (1965-90), he was involved in many missions overseas, from forging papers and documents to helping agents and others leave a country without detection. Famously, in 1980, in an audacious rescue, he disguised six American diplomats in Iran as a Canadian crew making a movie, so that they could be smuggled out of the country.

▼ A spy photographs sensitive documents using a miniature spy camera. Spies often pass on photos, objects, or documents to another agent, called a courier, who ferries this material back to the intelligence agency.

LOOK CLOSER

Pham Xuan An was a journalist in South Vietnam throughout the Vietnam War but actually spied for its enemy, North Vietnam. His rolls of film were often hidden inside spring rolls!

SPY STORIES

I N 1821, JAMES FENIMORE COOPER WROTE THE FIRST ESPIONAGE NOVEL, *THE SPY*. HARDLY ANYONE READ IT.

Today, millions enjoy books featuring spies such as James Bond, George Smiley, Jack Ryan, and teenage agent Alex Rider. Millions more are thrilled by TV shows that include *24* and *Alias*, or films such as the Bourne trilogy, *Spy Kids*, and the Bond movies.

The world of fictional spies is glamorous and action-packed, but the most successful real spies may remain unknown to all except their handlers until long after their deaths. Fictional spies are shown as all-rounders and loners. Real spies often work as part of a team, specializing in a field such as surveillance.

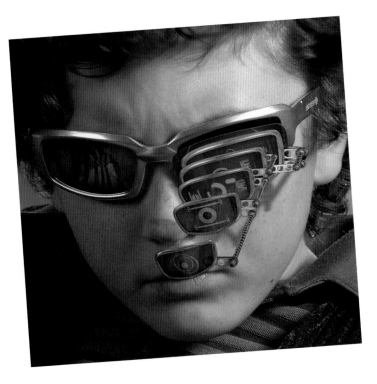

▲ *Juni Cortez (played by actor Daryl Sabara) in* Spy Kids 2 *uses a high-tech viewing device built into a pair of glasses. Spy films and books are often full of outrageous gadgets, some of which exist in real-life espionage.*

▼ *In a 2008 movie remake of the 1960s spy TV series,* Get Smart, *Steve Carell stars as bumbling secret agent Maxwell Smart, alongside Anne Hathaway.*

FACT OR FICTION?

S ome former agents have claimed that both the KGB and CIA read spy books and watched spy films to get ideas for real-life missions. Sometimes the spies gave ideas to writers. CIA director Allen Dulles provided plot ideas to popular spy story writer, Helen MacInnes. In spying, truth can sometimes be stranger than fiction. The human torpedo that Ian Fleming wrote about in **Thunderball** was based on a real Italian device used during World War II. Projects used by intelligence organizations during the Cold War included cigars filled with lethal explosives, a lipstick gun, and a live cat fitted with a radio inside its body and an aerial running up its tail!

LOOK CLOSER

Former **KGB** spy Oleg Gordievsky claimed that, when working for the **USSR** in London, he was ordered to obtain copies of the latest Bond movies for Soviet spies to study.

▲ Daniel Craig plays James Bond in the 2008 film Quantum of Solace. It is the 22nd official movie featuring the fictional British spy, James Bond, who has the code number 007 and is licensed to kill.

IAN FLEMING (1908-1964)
Fleming was a member of British naval intelligence during World War II. He created his ruthless secret agent, James Bond, in a series of 12 influential novels, the first being *Casino Royale* in 1952. Fleming took inspiration for his character from various sources including the real-life wartime spies, Dušan Popov and William Stephenson.

The Bible tells how God told Moses to send men ahead to spy out the land. Two of the spies, Joshua and Caleb (right), brought back the news that the land of Canaan was "rich with milk and honey."

THE FIRST SPIES

Knowing an Enemy

SPYING HAS EXISTED EVER SINCE PEOPLE HAVE FOUGHT WARS. SPYING IS ABOUT SECRETS. NOTHING IS MORE CRUCIAL TO WINNING A WAR THAN KNOWING THE PLANS OF AN ENEMY.

THE ART OF WAR

SPIES WERE USED IN ANCIENT INDIA, CHINA, EGYPT, AND ELSEWHERE TO SCOUT TERRITORY, INFILTRATE THE ENEMY, AND TO DECEIVE AND SPREAD LIES. THE BIBLE MENTIONS 12 SPIES, AMONG THEM CALEB AND JOSHUA WHO SPIED ON JERICHO FOR MOSES.

The first time spying techniques, known as spycraft, were written down was around 2,500 years ago. Sun Tzu's *The Art of War* described five types of spy, including inward spies (spies who worked for the enemy's ruler or court) and doomed spies (who were sacrificed). He urged the use of spies in all situations as a leader's eyes and ears.

LOOK CLOSER

In The Art of War, Sun Tzu tells the tale of spy and envoy Li I-Chi, who gave false information to the king of Ch'i. Li I-Chi was a "doomed spy" – in 203 BCE, he was boiled alive!

CUNEIFORM CODE

The Ancient Sumerians developed a writing system called cuneiform around 5,000 years ago. Few could read its symbols sculpted on clay tablets with a reed stylus. This meant that any message could be carried in secret. Most of the messages were about military plans but some of them were industrial secrets.

▲ Many believe Sun Tzu was a Chinese soldier or court official. His writings have influenced leaders as varied as Napoleon and US General Norman Schwarzkopf.

In 1274 BCE, the Hittite king, Muwatallis, sent two men to deceive the army of Pharaoh Rameses II.

The spies, disguised as Hittite deserters, convinced the pharaoh that the enemy were far away.

▼ Rameses II leads his soldiers in attack at the Battle of Kadesh (c.1274 BCE). Part of his army had nearly been ambushed because of the work of the Hittite spies. This event is the oldest recorded example of spies during wartime.

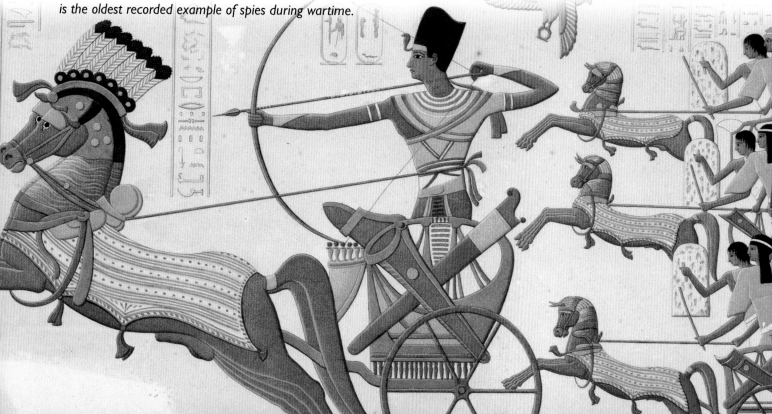

SPYING IN ANCIENT GREECE

ANCIENT GREECE WAS NOT A SINGLE COUNTRY. IT WAS DIVIDED UP INTO SMALL, INDEPENDENT LANDS THAT WERE CALLED CITY-STATES. THESE INCLUDED ATHENS, SPARTA, AND CORINTH.

Spying and plotting between the city-states and the neighboring Persian empire was rife. The Ancient Greeks split spying into two separate roles. Military scouts would find out the size of enemy shipping fleets and armies, the condition of roads and likely battlefields. Civilian spies were often merchants who worked and lived in enemy lands. Around 490 BCE, the Persian-controlled port of Sardis (in modern Turkey) was awash with civilian spies posing as merchants trying to find out the invasion plans of Xerxes, the leader of the Persians.

▲ This piece of pottery shows Darius I, ruler of the Persian empire, receiving a report from one of his spies.

SECRET MESSAGES

In the 5th century BCE, Demaratus, the Greek king of Sparta, hid a message on a wax tablet by scraping off the wax, writing a message on the wood underneath and then covering the message with a fresh layer of wax. The tablet traveled through the enemy's territory undetected. The scytale (see below) was another way of 'hiding' messages by scrambling up the order of the letters.

▼ First used in Sparta, the scytale or skytale was a leather strip or belt with letters branded or etched onto it. When wound round a pole of the right size, the letters lined up to spell out a secret message.

Histaeus of Miletus sent a message through enemy lands tattooed on a slave's head.

On arrival at his destination, the slave had a haircut to reveal the secret message.

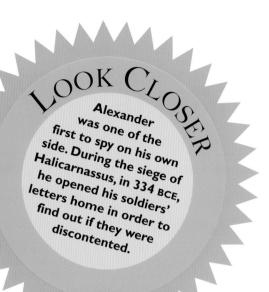

LOOK CLOSER

Alexander was one of the first to spy on his own side. During the siege of Halicarnassus, in 334 BCE, he opened his soldiers' letters home in order to find out if they were discontented.

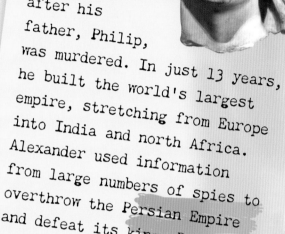

ALEXANDER THE GREAT

Alexander (356–323 BCE) took control of Macedon after his father, Philip, was murdered. In just 13 years, he built the world's largest empire, stretching from Europe into India and north Africa. Alexander used information from large numbers of spies to overthrow the Persian Empire and defeat its king, Darius III, at the Battle of Gaugamela.

▼ The Trojan Horse was a deadly gift. The Greek spy Sinon persuaded the Trojans to carry the horse inside the city walls. Hidden inside the horse were Greek soldiers, who opened the gates for the Greek army.

SPYING IN ANCIENT ROME

THE ROMAN EMPIRE STRETCHED ACROSS MUCH OF EUROPE, THE MIDDLE EAST, AND NORTH AFRICA. THE ROMANS PRIDED THEMSELVES ON A RUTHLESS AND EFFICIENT ARMY, BUT BEHIND THE SCENES, SPIES WERE AT WORK.

Roman spies came into their own in the Second Punic War (218–201 BCE) between Rome and Carthage (in modern Tunisia). Publius Cornelius Scipio was placed in charge of the Roman armies.

He used spies to defeat the Carthaginian commander Hannibal decisively at the Battle of Zama in 202 BCE. Back in Rome, plotting and dirty tricks were rife. There was no empire-wide intelligence system, but wealthy and powerful Roman families often kept their own network of private informers, agents, and couriers.

In the 1st century BCE, Marcus Crassus was a powerful Roman general and politician.

He cultivated useful contacts and built the largest personal spy network in Europe.

He used his spies to get news before anyone else and became the richest man in Rome.

◀ Hannibal, shown mounted on an elephant, battles with a Roman legion in the Alps. Hannibal placed spies in Roman army camps as well as Rome itself during the Second Punic War. This helped him win many victories, including the Battle of Cannae where 60,000 Roman soldiers died.

▲ *By the 1st century CE, frumentarii – soldiers who traveled to organize major army supplies – had been turned by their leaders into a dreaded secret police force, spying on local peoples, officials, and other Roman soldiers.*

▶ *Julius Caesar conquered Gaul, invaded Britain, and became absolute ruler of Rome. He organized a system of personal spies. It is said he was handed intelligence about a plot against him, on the very day he was assassinated in 44 BCE.*

THE CAESAR CIPHER

According to the Roman historian Suetonius, Julius Caesar used a simple substitution cipher to communicate with his generals. He shifted the letters of the message three letters further along the alphabet so that D in the secret message meant A, and E meant B and so on.

U H W X U Q W R U R P H
R E T U R N T O R O M E

MEDIEVAL SPYING

SPYING IN THE MEDIEVAL PERIOD VARIED GREATLY. IN MANY OF THE EUROPEAN COUNTRIES, IT WAS SMALL-SCALE AND LOCAL. RULERS IN THE MONGOL EMPIRE AND THE ARAB WORLD HAD LARGER SPY NETWORKS.

Spies in medieval Europe were mainly used to root out threats to a ruler – which sometimes came from within the royal family – and in battles. Spies called heralds were used to spot enemy knights on the battlefield. Other spies worked as monks, traders, or wandering minstrels – jobs that allowed them to move from place to place without causing suspicion.

When European forces invaded the Middle East during the Crusades they came up against Arab leaders called caliphs who had vast spy networks, often managed by an official called a kharbar. The Caliph of Baghdad had over 1,600 women spies.

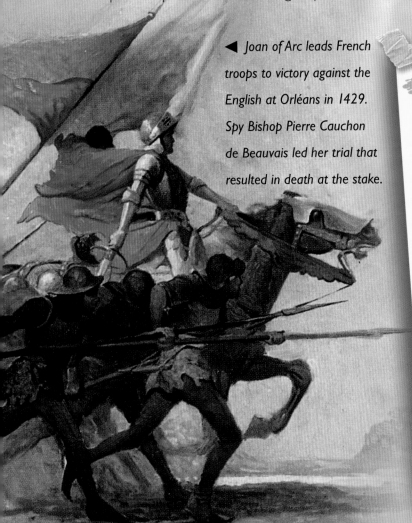

◄ *Joan of Arc leads French troops to victory against the English at Orléans in 1429. Spy Bishop Pierre Cauchon de Beauvais led her trial that resulted in death at the stake.*

ENTERTAINING THE ENEMY

Alfred the Great (c.849–899) was ruler of the Anglo-Saxon kingdom of Wessex in southern England. In around 878, with his kingdom under threat from invading Danes led by Guthrum, Alfred chose to become a spy himself. He posed as a wandering minstrel and entered the camp of the Danes. Alfred spent a week entertaining the enemy while spying on their numbers. His forces went on to defeat the Danes decisively at the Battle of Edington in 878.

▼ *Genghis Khan (c.1167–1227) brought together the warring Mongol tribes. He began a period of expansion that would create one of the world's largest empires. At its peak, the Mongol empire stretched from eastern China to the River Danube in Europe.*

▲ *A group of minstrels entertain a German ruler. Minstrels wandered from town to town singing songs and poems to important nobles and kings. This work provided an excellent cover for them to learn secrets.*

In Khan's empire, food, shelter, and fresh horses were supplied to messengers every 40km.

This meant Genghis Khan could receive intelligence very quickly and act on it.

FITTING IN

Trusted Mongol spies were sent ahead of invading armies to scout the land. They posed as camel-leaders and merchants. But the further away from Mongolia the empire expanded, the more the Mongols used locals as spies because they were less likely to be detected.

THE NINJA

I N MEDIEVAL JAPAN, GROUPS OF PAID SPIES, SCOUTS, AND ASSASSINS STRUCK TERROR INTO THE HEARTS OF THEIR ENEMIES. THEY WERE THOUGHT OF AS MAGICIANS AND INVISIBLE WARRIORS, AND WERE KNOWN AS *SHINOBI* OR *NINJA*.

No one knows how or when the first ninja came on the scene, but the warriors were at their most active in the Sengoku or warring states period (roughly 1460 – 1610). The ninja were often in the service of powerful warlords called *daimyo*, who asked them to carry out all kinds of missions. These included spying on enemy castles and battlegrounds, and assassinating rivals for power. Although they are known for all-black clothing, ninja would also wear all-white outfits to merge with snow or disguise themselves as wandering mountain monks (*yamobushi*). A monk's long robes would easily conceal a range of weapons.

THE ART OF STEALTH

N inja (written in Japanese kanji characters above) were people who practiced ninjutsu which means "the skill of going unperceived" or "the art of stealth." Training began in childhood. Adult ninja were skilled climbers, gymnasts, swimmers, and warriors. They used disguises, moved stealthily without making a sound and entered and left heavily guarded buildings without leaving a trace. Many Japanese people believed they had the power of invisibility.

▶ *A ninja master poses wearing typical black clothing. Underneath, he may wear lightweight body armor made of metal panels sewn into cloth. The handle of his razor-sharp sword contains poisons and antidotes.*

Ninja would enter an enemy castle secretly the night before a major battle.

They would light fires, harass the enemy, and steal the castle's banner or flag.

▶ *Jiralya the Magician (here riding on a toad) was a fictional outlaw from Japan, who possessed many of the powers of the ninja, including the ability to move silently.*

LOOK CLOSER

Many ninja carried a box of cricket insects. The chirping sounds the crickets made would cover any slight sounds the ninja made as they advanced stealthily.

▲ *A ninja safehouse was packed with defenses. If the headquarters was attacked, there were secret sliding wall panels, hidden staircases, trapdoors, and handholds on the walls and ceiling for a ninja to hang from.*

The ninja learned how to live off the land as they journeyed. Their training emphasized how many everyday things could be used to help them on their missions. They knew which plants could be eaten or used as a medicine or poison. A simple hollow river reed could be used as a blowpipe to fire a poison dart, or as a breathing straw should the ninja need to hide underwater. Even the long sash they wore around their waist had multiple uses. It could become a climbing rope when tied to a *kaginawa* (grappling hook) or a weapon to strangle a victim silently. It could also be woven between branches of trees to form a spider web hammock to sleep safely above ground.

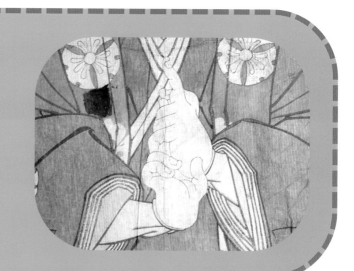

Tegaki claws

▲ Tegaki *claws could be worn on the hands or feet. They, along with* hokode *hand claws, were made of iron and used to climb castle walls or for close combat.*

Hokode claws

LOOK CLOSER

Many ninja threw egg shells filled with dust and ash called metsubushi (eye-closers). These blinded guards or created a smoke screen, allowing the ninja to slip past or escape.

SECRET FINGER SIGNS

The ninja concentrated their energy and thoughts before a mission with the help of a series of secret hand and finger signs called kuji-in. *These had been developed from Buddhist meditation techniques. In combat, the ninja would channel their energy into attack by making a roaring sound with their eyes blazing. This was called a* kiaijutsu, *meaning "spirited shout."*

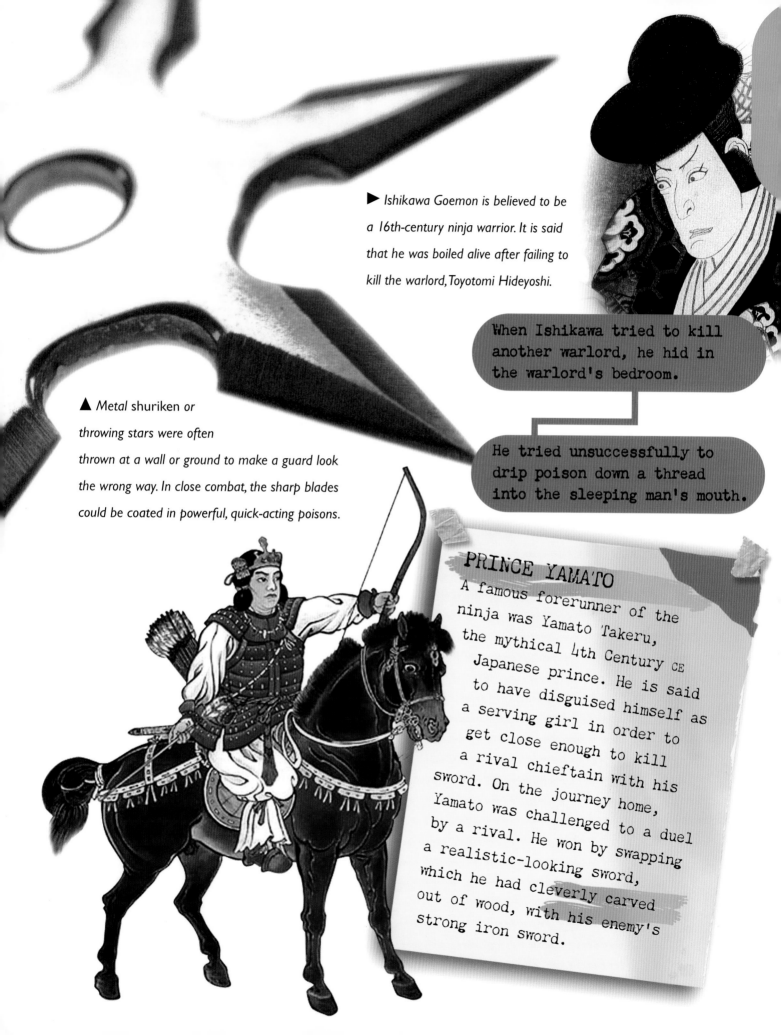

▶ Ishikawa Goemon is believed to be a 16th-century ninja warrior. It is said that he was boiled alive after failing to kill the warlord, Toyotomi Hideyoshi.

When Ishikawa tried to kill another warlord, he hid in the warlord's bedroom.

He tried unsuccessfully to drip poison down a thread into the sleeping man's mouth.

▲ Metal shuriken or throwing stars were often thrown at a wall or ground to make a guard look the wrong way. In close combat, the sharp blades could be coated in powerful, quick-acting poisons.

PRINCE YAMATO

A famous forerunner of the ninja was Yamato Takeru, the mythical 4th Century CE Japanese prince. He is said to have disguised himself as a serving girl in order to get close enough to kill a rival chieftain with his sword. On the journey home, Yamato was challenged to a duel by a rival. He won by swapping a realistic-looking sword, which he had cleverly carved out of wood, with his enemy's strong iron sword.

Events such as this ball at the court of Henry III of France were perfect for spies, mingling with the guests and servants of the king, to gather intelligence.

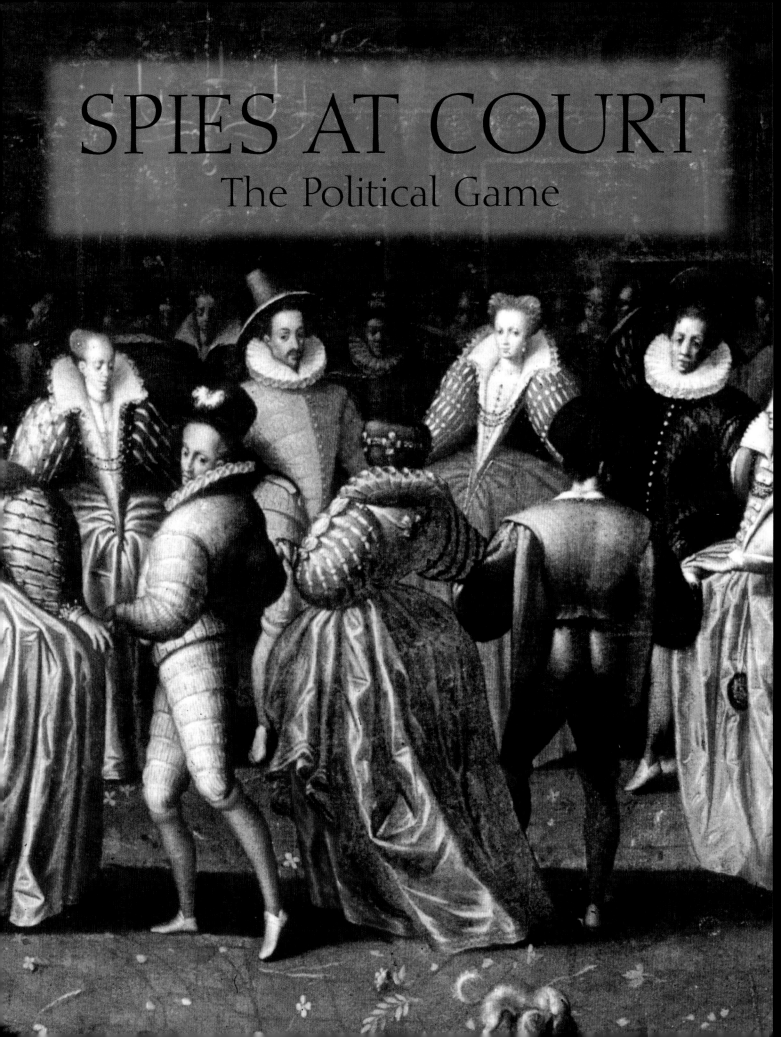

SPIES AT COURT
The Political Game

IN EUROPE IN THE 15TH TO 18TH CENTURIES THERE WERE FEW MORE DANGEROUS PLACES FOR A SPY TO BE THAN IN THE COURT OF A RIVAL KING. HE OR SHE RISKED CERTAIN DEATH IF THEY WERE DISCOVERED.

POLITICAL SPIES

EUROPE AT THIS TIME WAS A HOTBED OF INTRIGUE. DOZENS OF KINGS, QUEENS, NOBLES, AND WARLORDS VIED FOR INFLUENCE AND SENT THEIR SPIES TO THE COURTS OF OTHER POWERS.

Many spies were diplomats sent to build alliances or make agreements on trade or war. If they learned anything secret, they would send the information back by messenger. One diplomat for the Italian city-state of Florence, Niccolò Machiavelli, wrote books called *The Prince* and *On The Art Of War*. In these he argued that, for a ruler, "it is far safer to be feared than loved." He explained how messages could be baked in loaves of bread or put in the collars of hunting dogs.

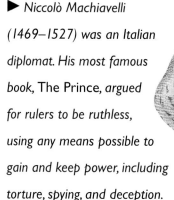

LOOK CLOSER

Prussian ruler Frederick the Great wrote a whole book arguing against Machiavelli. He was, however, in favor of spying, writing, 'I always march with one cook and a hundred spies.'

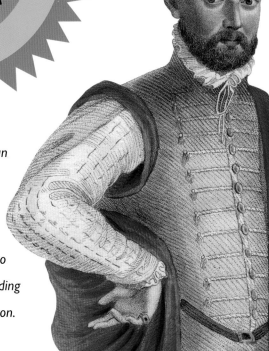

▶ *Niccolò Machiavelli (1469–1527) was an Italian diplomat. His most famous book,* The Prince, *argued for rulers to be ruthless, using any means possible to gain and keep power, including torture, spying, and deception.*

▲ Bertrand du Guesclin kneels before the French king Charles V. Du Guesclin was a valued knight and spy. When he was captured in 1364, Charles paid 100,000 francs for his freedom.

THE CIPHER WHEEL

The city-states of Italy were the center of new code-making devices, such as Leon Battista Alberti's polyalphabetic cipher disc (right). This featured a fixed outer ring of letters and a movable inner ring. If the cipher was the letter "g," you turned the inner circle to align the "g" to "A" on the outer circle. You decoded the message by finding the letters on the outer circle and writing the matching letters from the inner circle.

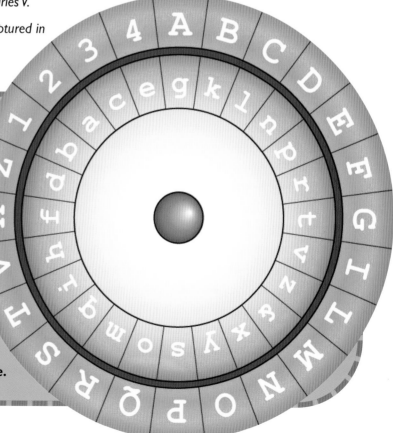

THE BABINGTON PLOT

GOOD QUEEN BESS WAS LOVED BY MANY OF HER SUBJECTS, BUT BEHIND THE SCENES THERE WERE MANY PLOTS AFOOT — NONE POTENTIALLY MORE DEADLY THAN THE BABINGTON PLOT.

As a Protestant queen, Elizabeth I (1533–1603) was constantly in danger from Catholics supported by Spain and other European Catholic powers. However, she had a powerful ally in the form of Sir Francis Walsingham, England's first great spymaster.

Walsingham was a passionate Protestant and hated Elizabeth's cousin Mary, Queen of Scots, who was a Catholic. Mary had been imprisoned since 1568 because of plots to remove Elizabeth from power. To convince Elizabeth to have Mary executed, Walsingham needed evidence of her direct involvement in a plot.

In 1585, Gilbert Gifford, a trainee priest, was captured as he came ashore from a boat that had carried him from France. Taken to Walsingham, Gifford confessed to being a messenger between Mary and her supporters. He agreed to become a double agent, passing all secret messages to Walsingham.

> Every week a barrel of beer was sent to Mary, with a hidden letter inside.

> Mary hid her reply in a waterproof package fixed in the bung hole of the barrel.

> She did not know that this "secret" system was one of Walsingham's clever ideas!

▶ *Elizabeth I wears a cloak embroidered with eyes and ears to signify her all-seeing and all-hearing intelligence operation.*

▲ Babington and 13 other conspirators were all executed in 1586. The following year, Mary (here played by Samantha Morton in the film Elizabeth: The Golden Age) was put on trial for treason and beheaded in February, 1587.

THE SECRET MESSAGES

Mary and Babington used substitution ciphers, where a letter of a message is substituted by a different letter, number, or symbol. Their letters had 23 symbols for letter substitutions and 36 characters for words and phrases. Walsingham's secretary, Thomas Phelippes, was an expert code-breaker who understood that certain letters appeared frequently in English – for example, E comprises 13 percent of all the letters in a message. Walsingham's operatives decoded the messages, and then faked the original seals and sent the letters on their way.

FRANCIS WALSINGHAM

The spymaster served his queen loyally for more than 20 years. He ran a very effective spy ring on Elizabeth's behalf, with agents in every court in Europe. His network of spies, heavy use of code-breaking, and, sometimes, torture enabled him to keep Elizabeth safely on the throne.

SPYING FOR FRANCE

IN THE 17TH AND 18TH CENTURIES, FRANCE BUILT ONE OF THE MOST NOTORIOUS SPY NETWORKS IN EUROPE. CARDINAL RICHELIEU AND HIS SUCCESSOR AS CHIEF MINISTER, MAZARIN, USED SPIES TO TURN FRANCE INTO A DOMINANT POWER.

French intelligence managed to place many spies in positions of trust in other countries. Richelieu's most effective spy was a monk called Father Joseph, whose real name was François Leclerc du Tremblay. In 1630, du Tremblay convinced the Austrian Habsburg Empire to dismiss its best general, Albrecht von Wallenberg. Then he persuaded Sweden to attack the weakened Austrians!

ADVENTURER AND SPY

Giacomo Casanova (1725–98) was infamous as a gambler, adventurer, and seducer of women. During his eventful life, he was recruited as an undercover agent by François de Bernis, the French foreign minister. Casanova used all his charm and persuasion not only to spy on British naval ships moored at Dunkirk, but to be invited to dine with the ships' captains on-board.

▲ The Palace of Versailles was where King Louis XV held top-secret government meetings. Louis established a cabinet noir – an espionage network, headed by Robert Jeannel, that spied on, and opened, read, and resealed the letters of nobles and foreign visitors.

CHEVALIER D'EON

France needed a spy deep inside Russia to forge an alliance. This almost impossible task was achieved by a masterspy, the Chevalier d'Eon. Disguised as a woman, he became a maid-in-waiting to Russian ruler Tsarina Elizabeth, and convinced her to sign a treaty with France. He later served as a soldier and expert swordsman, and a minister and spy for France in London.

▶ Armand-Jean du Plessis (1585–1642) became Cardinal Richelieu, the all-powerful first minister to Louis XIII. His network of spies inside France protected the king and his own position, and was built on during the reigns of Louis XIV and Louis XV.

LOOK CLOSER

When Tsarina Elizabeth discovered that her lady-in-waiting was a male spy, she offered the Chevalier d'Eon a high-ranking position. He refused but was allowed to return to France.

MASTER OF EUROPE

NAPOLEON BONAPARTE (1769–1821) DISCOVERED ON HIS FIRST CAMPAIGN THAT SPIES WERE VERY EFFECTIVE AT INTELLIGENCE GATHERING.

Napoleon established an efficient network of spies right across Europe, and selected and managed them himself. The gathered information brought him great success in many of his military campaigns. He also used the spies to help him politically. The spies found out what his opponents were saying so that Napoleon could take action against them. And he used spies as a security force for protection, surviving assassination attempts on several occasions.

Napoleon was heard to tell his followers that "gold is the only suitable reward for spies."

This gave him the perfect excuse when he refused to give the Légion d'Honneur to Schulmeister.

◀ The intelligence from spying helped Napoleon plan his strategy. In 1805, it helped him gain victory at the Battle of Austerlitz.

BREAKING NAPOLEON'S CODES

George Scovell was a low-ranking British officer on the Duke of Wellington's staff. He was brave in battle but forgotten when it came to promotion. However, it was he who broke the French codes in Spain during the Peninsular War. It was because of his work that the British were able to gain advantage over Napoleon at the Battle of Salamanca in July 1812.

LOOK CLOSER

By the time Napoleon came to power, spies who were suspected of being military personnel in disguise were being shot without trial.

MILITARY INTELLIGENCE

One of Napoleon's most successful agents was Karl Schulmeister (1770–1853). He infiltrated the Austrian army and gained the ear of its commander, Mack von Leiberich. Schulmeister was able to feed the Austrians false information in letters and specially printed French newspapers that stated that the French army was weak. Mack made mistakes as a result and was defeated at Ulm in 1805. When Napoleon captured the Austrian city of Vienna, he made Schulmeister the city's chief of police.

SECRET POLICE FORCE

Napoleon asked the diplomat Joseph Fouché, duc d'Otrante (1758–1820), to organize a secret police force for him. Fouché had been educated to be a priest but had never taken his vows. He developed a spy network for Napoleon that flourished throughout Europe. He arranged for enemies to be discredited, or sometimes even kidnapped and shot.

◄ Fouché had a reputation as a ruthless and ambitious man.

On 25 December 1776, George Washington, using very good intelligence from his network of spies, crossed the River Delaware and took the enemy by surprise at the Battle of Trenton.

REVOLUTIONARY SPIES

The American War of Independence

IN THE 18TH AND 19TH CENTURIES, THE OLD ORDER WAS **OVERTURNED.** SOME NEW COUNTRIES GAINED **INDEPENDENCE** AND SOME OLD ONES REMOVED THEIR **KING** OR **QUEEN** AS RULER.

PATRIOTS AND LOYALISTS

B Y THE MID-1770S, THE PEOPLE LIVING IN THE 13 ESTABLISHED COLONIES IN NORTH AMERICA HAD HAD ENOUGH OF BEING RULED BY THE BRITISH.

The American Revolution or War of Independence (1775–83) split the colonists. Some remained loyal to the British, who sent large forces to quell the revolution. Others, called patriots, favored independence. The British relied on loyalist spies. These included Ann Bates, a schoolteacher who posed as a pedlar and sold thread and needles to American army camps while secretly counting their numbers and weapons. The patriots, led by George Washington, worked hard to get their own spies close to or inside the British high command and army camps.

LOOK CLOSER
Nathan Hale went behind enemy lines in New York posing as a schoolteacher. Young, tall, and with scars on his face from an explosion, he was spotted and captured.

INVENTIVE PATRIOT CODES

The patriots used invisible inks, ciphers (pictured), and all kinds of codes. Spy Anna Smith Strong of New York used her clothesline. A black petticoat meant that agent Caleb Brewster had arrived by sea. The number of white handkerchiefs would show in which of the six bays nearby he was hiding.

▲ A British officer has tea with a woman not knowing that she is a patriot spy hoping to learn secrets. The patriot forces commanded by George Washington became highly skilled at securing information from the enemy.

▼ Spy Nathan Hale was one of Washington's first secret agents. He was captured and hanged in 1776. His last words were "I only regret that I have but one life to give my country."

ARNOLD AND ANDRÉ

Benedict Arnold was a brilliant commander for the patriots but, deep in debt and passed over for promotion, he switched sides. The patriots learned of his treachery when a British spy, Major John André, was captured carrying Arnold's plans in his boot. André was hanged, but Arnold escaped.

AMERICA'S FIRST SPYMASTER

THE BRITISH WERE CONFIDENT OF VICTORY DURING THE AMERICAN WAR OF INDEPENDENCE. THEY HAD NOT RECKONED WITH THE SKILLED SPYING AND TACTICS OF AMERICA'S COMMANDER-IN-CHIEF, THE MAN WHO WOULD BECOME THE FIRST AMERICAN PRESIDENT – GEORGE WASHINGTON.

Washington had learned hard lessons about the value of intelligence in 1755 when he was an aide to a British general when England was fighting France. The well-informed French knew where the British were, and ambushed and routed them. Two decades later, fighting against the British, Washington established many spies and spy rings. Some proved highly successful, especially at passing misinformation (lies made to look like the truth) to the British.

▶ *Washington copied out reports about troop numbers, exaggerating his forces by four or five times. He then let his assistant, Major John Clark, pass the false information to the British, who believed it.*

PATRIOT CUNNING

John Honeyman escaped from a patriot guardhouse using a key given to him by Washington and dodging a hail of gunfire aimed to miss. Appearing to be a daring loyalist, he gained the confidence of the enemy and convinced them that Washington planned to attack over Christmas, 1776. This misinformation laid the ground for Washington and his troops to emerge victorious at the Battle of Trenton.

▶ The British forces surrender, handing over the sword of their leader, Lord Cornwallis, at Yorktown in 1781. Cornwallis had stayed in New York to defend against a major attack – a false rumor circulated by Washington's spies. Yorktown was the last major battle of the war, which ended in independence for America in 1783.

LOOK CLOSER

America's first organized spying force were the Knowlton Rangers, led by Thomas Knowlton. They were formed in 1776, but Knowlton was killed in battle the same year.

THE CULPER SPY RING

Washington recruited Benjamin Tallmadge (right), a former classmate of Nathan Hale, to head the Culper Spy Ring in 1778. Based in New York, at the heart of the British forces, the spy ring's missions ranged from sabotage (burning 300 tons of hay stored for British army horses) to alerting Washington that the British intended to attack ships that were bringing him reinforcements.

In the 1860s, the Union in the northern United States and the Confederates in the south (pictured here) used intelligence in their fight against each other.

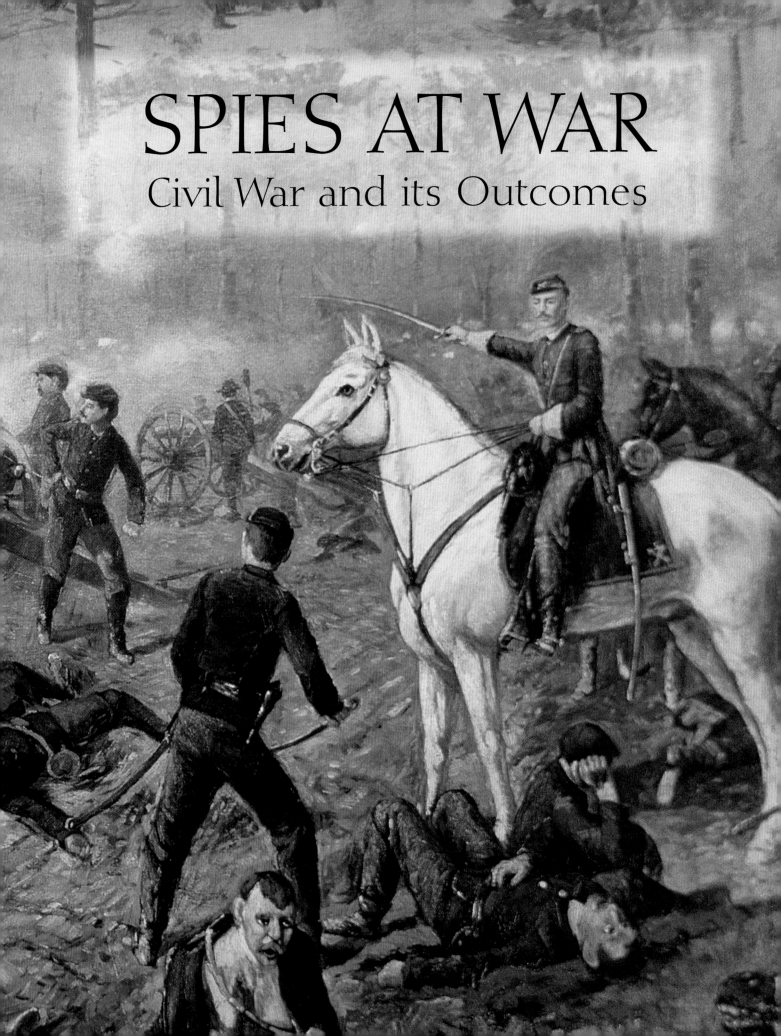

SPIES AT WAR
Civil War and its Outcomes

SEVERAL SAVAGE

WARS RAGED

DURING THE 19TH

CENTURY. SPIES

ON ALL SIDES

PLAYED

THEIR PART IN

GAINING

INFORMATION

THAT SOMETIMES

MADE A VITAL

DIFFERENCE.

BATTLES FOR TERRITORY

WARS IN AFRICA, THE UNITED STATES, AND EUROPE SAW THOUSANDS OF SPIES IN ACTION. SOME WERE EQUIPPED WITH EXCITING NEW INVENTIONS SUCH AS PHOTOGRAPHY AND THE TELEGRAPH.

The American Civil War (1861–65) was the largest of these conflicts. It was fought between the 11 states of the south (the Confederates) and the 23 states of the north, which remained in the Union. At issue was the use of slaves, on which the south's economy was dependent. At the same time, the Crimean War (1853–56) and the "scramble for Africa" (1880s–1914) saw European countries fighting for the control of territory.

LOOK CLOSER

Invented in the 1840s, the telegraph allowed messages to be sent quickly over long distances. During the Second Boer War in South Africa, both sides used telegraphy.

SPY BALLOONS

Balloons were used in many wars, including Professor Thaddeus Lowe's Intrepid (right) during the American Civil War. The British used balloon squadrons in the Boer War (1880–81) to spot Boer soldiers hiding in the rough terrain. During the Franco-Prussian War (1870–71), the French used balloons for spying, and sending and receiving important messages.

▲ In the 1860s, photography was a novelty. Many soldiers, like these American Civil War artillerymen, were happy to pose. Little did they realize that some photographers were spies photographing their weapons and troop positions.

▼ The American Civil War saw the first battle fought between ironclad ships – the USS Monitor (left) and the CSS Virginia. The day before their confrontation in 1862, the Virginia had sunk two big Union warships, the Congress and the Cumberland.

Wilhelm Stieber was Prussia's leading spymaster. He first spied on communists in the 1850s.

By the outbreak of the Franco-Prussian War in 1870, Stieber had almost 40,000 spies in France.

Prussia won easily and Stieber left 15,000 spies in France, many disguised as farm workers.

UNION SPIES

AT THE START OF THE AMERICAN CIVIL WAR, THE UNION HAD NO ORGANIZED INTELLIGENCE FORCE. THE CONFEDERATE SOUTH WAS ABLE TO SPY AT WILL UNTIL THE UNION DEVELOPED ITS OWN EFFECTIVE SPYING NETWORKS.

Allan Pinkerton had run a national detective agency before the war. In 1861, he was appointed to run the Union Intelligence Service, which would later become the US Secret Service. Many of the Union spies uncovered little information or were quickly caught. However, one of Pinkerton's star agents, George Curtis, was never suspected as a spy. He managed to work his way into a position of trust in the Confederate capital of Richmond, Virginia, by posing as a merchant selling goods the Confederacy needed – anything from ammunition to quinine medicine.

> ► Allan Pinkerton sometimes spied using the alias Major E. J. Allen. He pioneered surveillance and other spying techniques.

Curtis was trusted by the Confederates with carrying important messages.

He passed the messages to his handler, George Bangs, who had the documents copied.

Curtis then collected the messages and delivered them to a Confederate general.

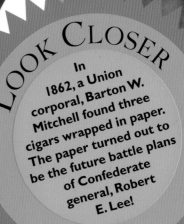

LOOK CLOSER

In 1862, a Union corporal, Barton W. Mitchell found three cigars wrapped in paper. The paper turned out to be the future battle plans of Confederate general, Robert E. Lee!

◄ Actress Pauline Cushman spied on General Bragg and his Confederate forces in Nashville in 1863. Captured and sentenced to death, she was saved just three days before her hanging by an invasion of Union forces.

HARRIET TUBMAN

Born a slave, Harriet Tubman (1821-1913) escaped her master in 1849 and then helped dozens of other slaves do the same. She provided intelligence that helped Colonel Montgomery capture Jacksonville in Florida. In 1863, she scouted the Combahee River in secret and guided three Union gunboats safely past mines to attack enemy plantations and free more than 700 slaves.

THE RICHMOND UNDERGROUND

Elizabeth Van Lew's family were well connected in the Confederate capital of Richmond. She was known locally as "Crazy Bet," but she actually ran a spy ring for the Union. Van Lew even managed to get her former black servant, Mary Bowser, placed in the home of the Confederate leader, Jefferson Davis. Bowser had a photographic memory and passed on information. Van Lew often hid important communications in everyday items such as eggs and jewelry.

▼ This beautiful ring is an example of the clever devices used by some of the Union spies. It has a concealed chamber for hiding secret messages.

SPYING FOR THE SOUTH

SOME OF THE MOST SUCCESSFUL SPIES IN HISTORY HAVE BEEN WOMEN. DURING THE AMERICAN CIVIL WAR, MANY WOMEN CLEVERLY AND BRAZENLY SPIED FOR THE CONFEDERATES IN THE SOUTH.

Women made very effective spies because they were often able to cross the lines without being suspected as they went about their daily business. Some were able to get close to Union command posts in their work as servants or nurses. Others hid Confederate soldiers or managed to courier important messages or medicines to the forces in the south. Many escaped detection altogether, and even those who were caught were usually only imprisoned for a short time.

ROSE O'NEAL GREENHOW

Rose was a socialite who counted the ex-president James Buchanan among her friends in Washington. She listened at functions and dinner parties, passing on information about any Union policies and military movements. She used two female couriers, Lillie MacKall and Betty Duvall, to ferry the information to the south.

TO CATCH A SPY

When Allan Pinkerton, head of the Union Secret Service, first suspected Rose Greenhow, she was taken to Old Capitol Prison (above) with her daughter, Little Rose. She was not the only female spy held there. The notorious Belle Boyd was there in 1862.

Some of Rose Greenhow's messages got through the lines inside buns of hair on her couriers' heads.

Lottie Moon dressed up as an old woman to carry information to General Kirby Smith.

When Lottie's sister Ginnie was caught, she swallowed the secret messages she was carrying.

◀ *Belle Boyd (1844–1900) served the Confederate forces in the Shenandoah Valley, operating from her father's hotel in Front Royal. She carried messages in a hollowed-out watch case.*

▲ *Rose Greenhow's information helped the Confederates, under brigadier generals Johnston and Beauregard, defeat the Union forces in the first Battle of Bull Run (above).*

LOOK CLOSER

On 23 May, 1862, Belle Boyd ran to greet General Stonewall Jackson's men, braving enemy fire. Despite bullet holes in her skirt, she managed to warn them of Union plans.

SPYING IN SOUTH AFRICA

D URING THE LATE 19TH CENTURY A MAJOR WAR BROKE OUT IN SOUTH AFRICA BETWEEN THE BRITISH SETTLERS AND DUTCH FARMERS, KNOWN AS BOERS IN THE REGION.

Britain was the world's leading superpower during this period, but the country spent just £20,000 a year on spying at the time and had few spies in other nations. When the Second Boer War (1899–1902) began, the Boer's secret service, De Geheime Dienst,

had established a cover for its spies in Britain as well as in African towns such as Pretoria, with its large number of British settlers. Britain had Frederick Russell Burnham, a resourceful American, on its side, and he headed the British network of battlefield scouts.

Frederick Russell Burnham taught many British scouts how to spy on enemy forces.

During the war, he and Frederick Duquesne (see p.51) had orders to assassinate one another.

▼ Boer troops crouch and aim during the Siege of Mafeking (1899–1900). British forces under Robert Baden-Powell held out for 221 days until reinforcements arrived.

LOOK CLOSER

When defending Mafeking against Boer attacks, Baden-Powell planted fake minefields. He got his troops to step over imaginary barbed wire to deceive the Boer spies.

▲ Baden-Powell's sketch of an ivy leaf is actually the map of the land and gun positions around a big fort. The shaded area shows where there is shelter from gunfire.

FREDERICK DUQUESNE

The story of South African spy Frederick Duquesne (1877-1956) reads like an adventure book. During the Second Boer War, he was wounded at the Battle of Ladysmith and captured twice, escaping both times. He joined the British army in Britain, posed as an officer, and was posted back to South Africa where he carried out sabotage missions against the British. Duquesne would spy for Germany against the British in both world wars.

BADEN-POWELL'S SKETCHES

Robert Baden-Powell (1857–1951) frequently used disguises to enable him to fool enemy sentries and obtain the information he wanted. According to his book, *My Adventures as a Spy*, he would sometimes pose as a naturalist making sketches of butterflies, leaves, and insects when all the time he was noting an enemy's defenses. He would later become famous as the founder of the Boy Scout movement.

▶ This portrait shows Robert Baden-Powell when he was lieutenant-general in the British Army in 1902, and stationed with the 13th Hussars at Kandahar in Afghanistan.

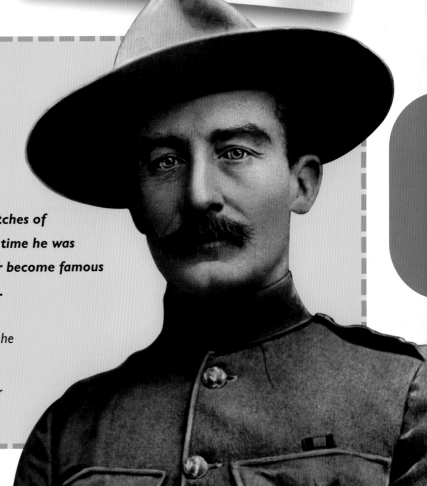

Allied soldiers man an anti-aircraft gun during World War I (1914–1918). They are in action near Frezenberg in Belgium during the 3rd Battle of Ypres, also known as the Battle of Passchendaele, in 1917.

WORLD WAR I
The War to End All Wars

WAR WAS

LOOMING

IN THE EARLY

20TH CENTURY AS

THE MAJOR POWERS

OF THE WORLD

JOSTLED FOR

SUPERIORITY. THE

TENSIONS

BETWEEN COUNTRIES

LED, IN 1914, TO

WORLD WAR I.

BEFORE THE WAR

TROUBLE STIRRED THROUGHOUT EUROPE AND ELSEWHERE AS COUNTRIES FORGED ALLIANCES. THEY ALL USED SPIES TO ALERT THEM TO ANY DEVELOPMENTS IN THE ARMIES AND NAVIES OF RIVAL COUNTRIES.

When Russia and Japan fought a war in 1904–5, all the major European powers sent their spies to observe the two nations. Japan's victory was, in part, due to its spies, led by Motojirÿo Akashi who had a massive war chest of one million yen. He used it to stir up trouble in Russia and to recruit super spies, including Sidney Reilly, to spy on the Russian fleet at Port Arthur, China.

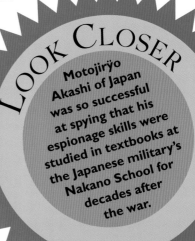

LOOK CLOSER

Motojirÿo Akashi of Japan was so successful at spying that his espionage skills were studied in textbooks at the Japanese military's Nakano School for decades after the war.

▼ *The Imperial Japanese Army are pictured, about to launch an attack on Russian troops at Port Arthur in 1904, just before they declared war on Russia.*

THE BLACK HAND GANG

The Black Hand Gang wanted independence for parts of Austria–Hungary's empire. Its leader, Dragutin Dimitrijevic, codename Apis, sent assassins into Sarajevo, Serbia in June 1914 to kill the heir to the throne of Austria, Archduke Franz Ferdinand. This event triggered the start of World War I.

Having failed to kill Archduke Ferdinand, the assassin Gavrilo Princip, went to a café to eat.

Ferdinand's car backed into the very same road, so Princip tried again and this time killed the Archduke!

▲ Japanese spies were not always successful during the 1904–5 Russo-Japanese war. This illustration, from a French magazine, shows two Japanese spies being hanged by Russian soldiers after they have been caught spying.

FRIENDS OR RIVALS?

Germany and Britain became fierce rivals in the early years of the 20th century. They both engaged in an arms race, building dozens of new warships while spying on each other. On one occasion, they worked together as German spy Gustav Steinhauer and Britain's William Melville cooperated to foil a plot to kill Germany's head of state, Kaiser Wilhelm, on his visit to Britain in 1901. Steinhauer would later be in command of many German spies working secretly in Britain.

▶ King Edward VII and Kaiser Wilhelm II on horseback at the state funeral of Queen Victoria in 1901.

ENEMY MOVEMENTS

WORLD WAR I BEGAN IN AUGUST 1914 WITH THE POWERFUL NATIONS OF EUROPE ALIGNED IN TWO GROUPS – THE CENTRAL POWERS (GERMANY, AUSTRIA-HUNGARY, BULGARIA, AND THE OTTOMAN EMPIRE) AND THE ALLIED POWERS (FRANCE, BRITAIN, BELGIUM, SERBIA, AND THE RUSSIAN EMPIRE).

In August 1914, Europe's large armies had to be mobilized. With forces of millions of men on the march, countries needed to know what other countries were doing. Some nations were already skilled in spying. Baron August Schluga, for example, was a German spy who had been undercover for decades. During World War I, he became known as Agent 17. This was because he managed to obtain the French Plan 17 for mobilizing its forces – a crucial secret.

▼ *German soldiers advance in 1914. In total, 65 million men served in armies during World War I, and around 10 million of them died.*

CHER AMI

Pigeons served as spies during the war, ferrying cameras in flight over enemy lines or carrying messages. The most famous of all was Cher Ami. At the Battle of Verdun in 1918, an American unit was trapped and threatened by its own side's artillery fire. Cher Ami carried a message back despite being blinded in one eye and hit by bullets in the chest and leg. Over 190 soldiers were saved as a result. Army medics carved the pigeon a wooden leg to replace the one lost.

◀ For the first time in a major conflict aircraft, like this Voisin V biplane, acted as spies in the sky, reporting on enemy positions and troop movements.

LOOK CLOSER

By 1915, cameras were being used in reconnaissance planes. The British estimated that their planes took half a million photographs from the air during World War I.

In 1914, a British aircraft spotted General von Kluck's German army moving to surround the British.

As a result, the British forces retreated toward Mons. As many as 100,000 lives were saved.

BLACKMAILED INTO BETRAYAL

The son of a poor railroadman, Alfred Redl became a colonel and head of the Austrian espionage service, the Kundschaftsstelle, in 1900. Shortly afterwards, Russian spies started to blackmail him about details of his private life. For around ten years before his capture and suicide in 1913, Redl was Russia's leading spy. He passed on Austria-Hungary's entire Plan III – the plan for how their armies would attack Serbia if war began. As a result, the Austrian army suffered a series of major defeats in 1914.

▶ Colonel Redl's intelligence helped the Serbians to defeat the Austro-Hungarian empire at the Battle of Cer, the first victory for the Allied Powers.

GERMAN SPIES ABROAD

AT 2.08 AM ON 30 JULY, 1916, A GIGANTIC EXPLOSION ROCKED NEW YORK AND NEW JERSEY, CAUSING MILLIONS OF DOLLARS OF DAMAGE. A DEPOT HOLDING AMMUNITION AND EXPLOSIVES BOUND FOR ALLIED FORCES IN EUROPE HAD BEEN SABOTAGED (RIGHT) BY GERMAN SPIES LIVING ABROAD.

German spies working in the United States sabotaged many ships and supplies heading for Britain and its allies. Germany was wary of Britain's navy, so the spies were dispatched to dockyards and harbors in England and Scotland. Two of them, Janseen and Loos, posed as Dutch salesmen and sent messages about the numbers and types of ships disguised as cigar orders. They were captured in 1915, by which time Germany had few spies left in Britain.

Jules Silber worked as a letters censor in Britain. He photographed messages and sent them to Germany.

It was only in 1925 that he revealed his spying when he published his memoirs.

THE SECRET SERVICE BUREAU

Public fears over Germany and German spies grew in the years before World War I. One British newspaper, The Weekly News, offered £10 to readers to write in to its "Spy Editor" and inform on Germans. In 1909, the British government set up the Secret Service Bureau. Major Vernon Kell led a team of just 14 staff. They caught more than 20 German spies between 1909 and 1914 and on the first day of the war captured over a dozen more. By the end of the war, the bureau, renamed MI5 in 1916, employed more than 850 people.

▼ Major Vernon Kell (left) leaves the War Office, where he had been discussing strategy.

▼ *New Yorkers survey the wreckage caused by the devastating explosion on Black Tom island in New York Harbor. It was one of over 50 acts of sabotage and many spying missions performed by German spies in the United States.*

COURTNEY DE RYSBACH

A popular music hall entertainer, de Rysbach was a German spy captured in July 1915. With telephone lines cut to Germany, de Rysbach had sent secret messages written between the lines of sheet music. He used an invisible ink made from potassium ferrocyanide mixed with toothpaste.

▼ *Many captured German spies were held in the Tower of London. In November 1914, Karl Lody was the first of 11 German spies to be executed – the first execution to take place there in more than 150 years.*

LOOK CLOSER

George Breeckow was the eighth German spy to be executed at the Tower of London. Notes on British military ships were written on thin rice paper hidden inside his shaving brush.

WOMEN AT WAR

URING WORLD WAR I, WOMEN MAINLY STAYED AWAY FROM THE FIGHTING. BUT MORE THAN 70,000 WOMEN DID SERVE AS NURSES AND ORDERLIES NEAR THE BATTLEFRONT, OR IN A FEW CASES, AS SPIES AND SPYMASTERS.

Many female spies, such as Mata Hari and Marthe Richer, were expected to become friends or lovers of important military figures to gain access to secrets. Others, such as Louise de Bettignes, helped run networks of agents in enemy territory.

Bettignes' main courier was Marie-Léonie Vanhoutte, who posed as a cheese seller to get through German lines. Vanhoutte had earlier worked with nurse Edith Cavell in Belgium. From 10 Rue Pepiniere, Antwerp, also in Belgium, Elsbeth Schragmuller taught spying as an academic subject, with strict training and exams.

LOOK CLOSER

Traveler Gertrude Bell was an expert on the Middle East. She became the only female officer in British intelligence during World War I.

Each of Schragmuller's trainee spies studied 12 hours a day, was known by a number and wore a mask.

The "final exam" was a mission in German-held territory. Failure meant being sent home.

◀ In the 1969 film about German spy Elsbeth Schragmuller, Fraulein Doktor, she spies against the Allies disguised as a nurse. German military intelligence destroyed almost all record of her.

◀ *The most infamous female spy of World War I, exotic dancer Mata Hari counted German, British, French, and Russian officers among her lovers. In 1917, the French executed her.*

MARTHE RICHER

One of France's first women pilots, Marthe Richer (1889–1982) was a double agent who spied for France. She was sent to Spain where she became the lover of a German admiral, Baron Hans von Krohn. She gave French intelligence details of where German U-boats refueled off the Spanish coast and the latest German spy technology, an invisible ink so powerful it was contained in a capsule the size of a grain of rice.

EDITH CAVELL

From late 1914 onward, British nurse Cavell hid over 200 Allied servicemen. She obtained identity papers and other forged documents, and helped guide the men through German occupied territory. She was shot as a spy in October 1915.

THE ZIMMERMANN TELEGRAM

IN JANUARY 1917, THE GERMAN FOREIGN MINISTER ARTHUR ZIMMERMANN SENT A TELEGRAM TO THE GERMAN AMBASSADOR TO MEXICO. ITS CONTENTS WERE EXPLOSIVE!

The telegram was sent via Washington on a cable line that was supposed to be used for peaceful purposes. It was intercepted by British Intelligence and decoded by their expert code-breakers. Germany was offering an alliance with Mexico to help it recapture territories lost in its war with the USA in 1848.

Zimmermann was also proposing that Mexico should get Japan involved in their fight with the USA.

The decoded telegram was released to the US press on 1 March. The public outcry was deafening. President Woodrow Wilson declared war on Germany, a decision approved by Congress on 6 April. The code-breakers had changed the course of history.

> The British broke the code in Room 40, in the Old Admiralty Building in London.

> One code-breaker had a bathtub installed in Room 40 - he did his best thinking in the bath!

▼ *On 7 May, 1915, the British liner Lusitania was torpedoed and sunk by a U-boat. The Germans stopped unrestricted submarine warfare shortly after for fear of causing US entry into the war.*

◀ *The telegram played a decisive role in the decision by the United States to enter the war.*

LOOK CLOSER

The Germans used a codebook with 10,000 number-coded words for the telegram. But the British had already decoded similar messages, so it did not take them long to decode this one.

ARTHUR ZIMMERMANN

After a career as a lawyer and diplomat, Zimmermann's time as Foreign Minister was short-lived. He had been appointed in November 1916 and was the first non-aristocrat to hold the post. The sending of the telegram certainly contributed to his resignation in August 1917.

SUBMARINE WARFARE

In the early months of 1915, Germans began to use unrestricted submarine warfare (USW). They planned to blockade and starve Britain into surrender by sinking without warning cargo ships bringing food and supplies to Britain. Based mainly off the Belgian coast, the U-boats, once submerged, evaded most patrols and were difficult to shell. Germany temporarily stopped USW not long after the sinking of the Lusitania, but began again in early 1917.

▼ *The U-boats were vulnerable on the surface or at periscope depth, when they could be rammed.*

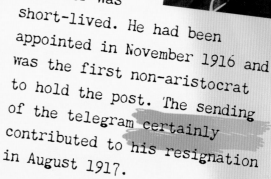

Parades in support of the communist government were frequent in Russia during the inter-war years. This youth demonstration on the streets of Moscow took place on 1 June, 1923.

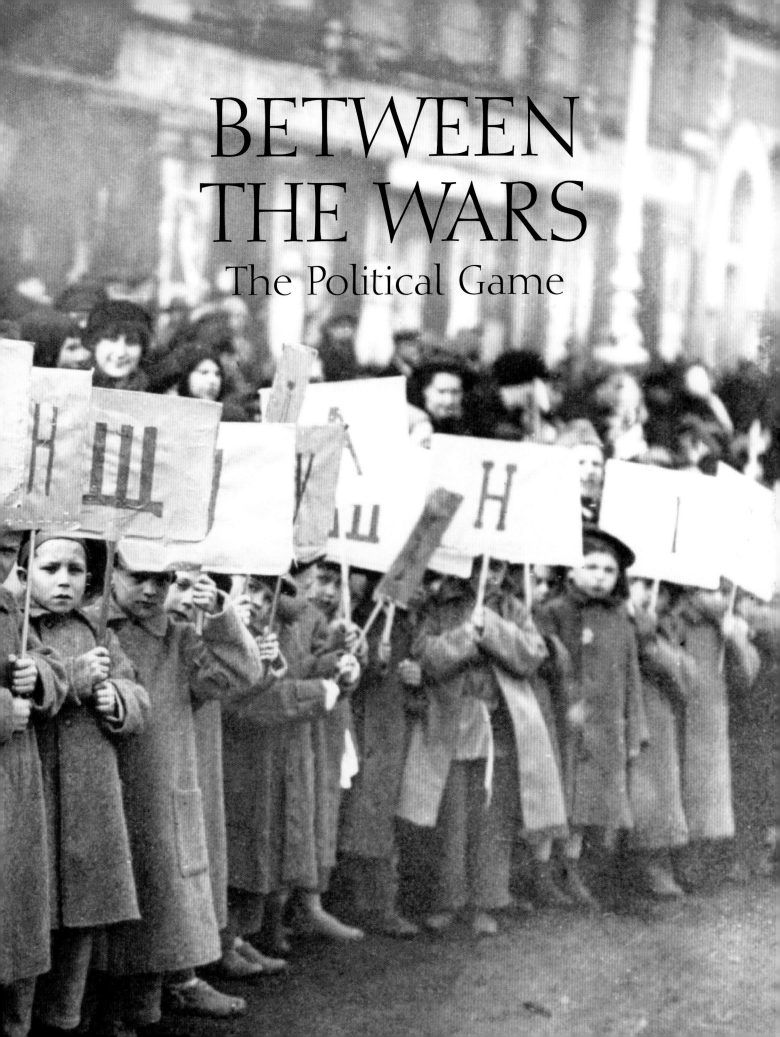

BETWEEN THE WARS
The Political Game

RUSSIA HAD BEEN RULED BY THE TSARS FOR 500 YEARS. BUT REVOLUTION BROUGHT BOLSHEVIK COMMUNISTS TO POWER IN 1917. FIVE YEARS LATER, RUSSIA WAS RENAMED THE SOVIET UNION.

THE BOLSHEVIK REVOLUTION

THE OKHRANA SECRET POLICE WERE FORMED AFTER THE ASSASSINATION OF TSAR ALEXANDER II IN 1881. THEIR DUTY WAS TO PROTECT RUSSIA'S ROYAL FAMILY BUT THEY SECRETLY ASSASSINATED IMPORTANT RUSSIAN MINISTERS, INCLUDING PRIME MINISTER PYOTR STOLYPIN IN 1911.

The Okhrana made great use of agent provocateurs – spies who influence an individual or infiltrate another group, persuading them to commit a crime. The Okhrana could not stop the Bolsheviks, led by Vladimir Lenin, in 1917. Russia was plunged into revolution and the Bolsheviks formed their own spying and secret police system which became known as the Cheka.

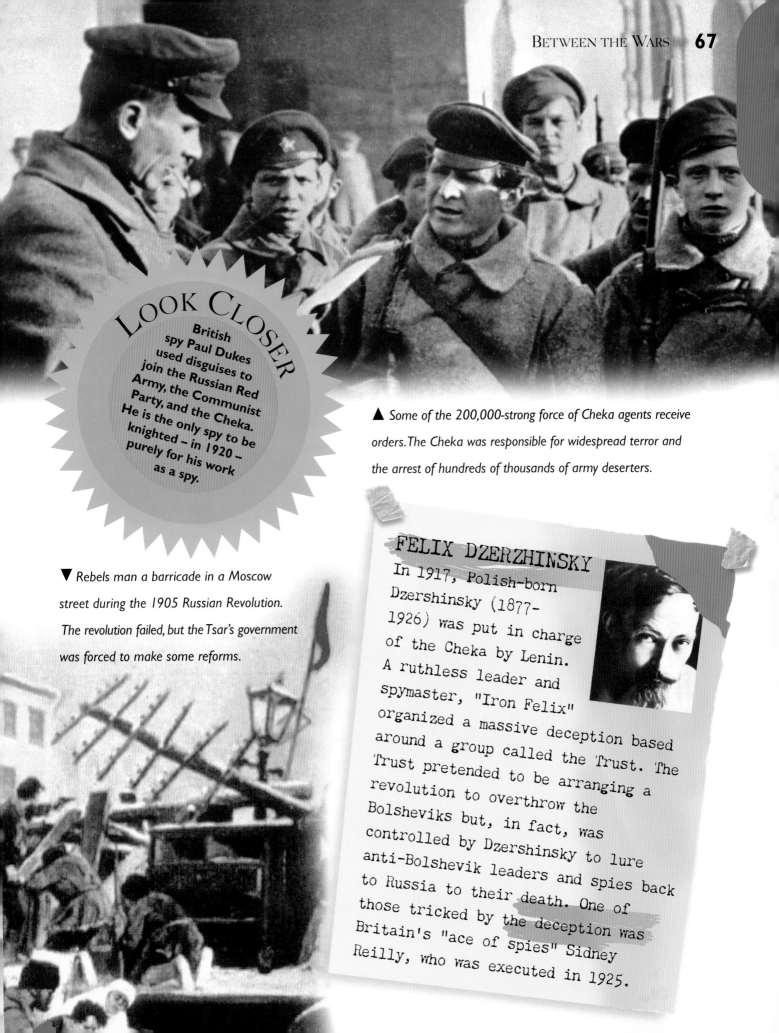

LOOK CLOSER

British spy Paul Dukes used disguises to join the Russian Red Army, the Communist Party, and the Cheka. He is the only spy to be knighted – in 1920 – purely for his work as a spy.

▲ Some of the 200,000-strong force of Cheka agents receive orders. The Cheka was responsible for widespread terror and the arrest of hundreds of thousands of army deserters.

▼ Rebels man a barricade in a Moscow street during the 1905 Russian Revolution. The revolution failed, but the Tsar's government was forced to make some reforms.

FELIX DZERZHINSKY

In 1917, Polish-born Dzershinsky (1877-1926) was put in charge of the Cheka by Lenin. A ruthless leader and spymaster, "Iron Felix" organized a massive deception based around a group called the Trust. The Trust pretended to be arranging a revolution to overthrow the Bolsheviks but, in fact, was controlled by Dzershinsky to lure anti-Bolshevik leaders and spies back to Russia to their death. One of those tricked by the deception was Britain's "ace of spies" Sidney Reilly, who was executed in 1925.

A Douglas SBD-3 flies away from the
burning Japanese carrier Akagi at the Battle
of Midway after emptying its bomb rack.

WORLD WAR II
Global Military Conflict

On 1 September, 1939, Germany invaded its neighbor, Poland. Two days later, France declared War on Germany. World War II had begun.

Germany Strikes

Germany's intelligence service, the Abwehr, led by Wilhelm Canaris, had small numbers of spies already in place at the outbreak of war.

These included spies at French cement works who stole the complete plans of France's forts and concrete defenses. There were also spies in Poland who fed false information that helped the German forces sweep through Poland with ease. Further afield, the Germans had infiltrated many spies into the United States, including the Duquesne Spy Ring, which numbered more than 30 agents. In Turkey, a humble valet, Elyesa Bazna, proved invaluable in cracking safes and stealing secrets from the British ambassador to that country.

Spies were not only operational on the ground. In 1939, the German LZ130 airship flew close to the coast of Britain in order to spy on the country's radar system.

▼ *Operation Bernhard was a German plan to ruin the British economy with thousands of fake British banknotes. The plan was not put into action but Germany did use the forged notes to pay for imports from other countries.*

▶ *The dome of St. Paul's Cathedral remains unscathed as London is bombed during the massive bombing campaign called the Blitz.*

In 1937, German spy Nikolaus Ritter successfully smuggled top secret drawings out of the USA.

The drawings of a new bombsight used by bomber planes were rolled up inside a hollow umbrella.

WHAT'S IN A DOT?

German spies made great use of microdot technology. Images or messages were shrunk by photography until they were a dot just a fraction of an inch across. Hundreds of microdots could be hidden in a hollowed-out ring on a finger or slid between the paper layers of a postcard. When the Allies discovered the first microdot in 1941, FBI director J. Edgar Hoover called them "the enemy's masterpiece of espionage."

▼ *This ordinary wristwatch holds a microdot carrying a top secret message in German.*

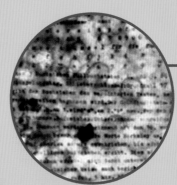

LOOK CLOSER

One German spy in the 1930s was a close friend of the British royal family. Leopold Gustav Alexander von Hoesch played tennis and golf with Britain's former king, Edward VIII.

THE RESISTANCE

DURING WORLD WAR II, THE RESISTANCE TO OCCUPATION BY GERMAN, ITALIAN, AND JAPANESE FORCES GREW IN COUNTRIES IN ASIA AND EUROPE. IT WAS AIDED BY INTELLIGENCE ORGANIZATIONS SUCH AS THE BRITISH SPECIAL OPERATIONS EXECUTIVE (SOE) AND THE AMERICAN OFFICE OF STRATEGIC SERVICES (OSS).

The feats of some resistance groups are still shrouded in secrecy today, but there were many famous successes. The French and Dutch resistance groups produced thousands of valuable pieces of intelligence, from German troop movements to plans of fortifications smuggled out by couriers or transmitted by radio. Yugoslavia's partisans, led by Josip Tito, became a major force of over half a million people who fought the Germans and their allies in the Balkans. They also helped more than 700 US airmen, who had been shot down, escape to safety. Greek resistance constantly harassed Italian troops, while OSS-trained Chinese and Vietnamese resistance workers spied on, and often fought, Japanese forces.

▼ *From the protection of a building, French snipers take aim at German troops. Harassing, sabotage, aiding escaping Allied servicemen, and spying on the Germans were all tasks carried out by members of the Resistance in France.*

LOOK CLOSER

The resistance in Norway spied on German ships and damaged Germany's atomic program. To identify themselves they wore paper clips on their jacket lapels.

RESISTANCE KIT

The SOE, OSS, and other intelligence organizations produced thousands of pieces of spy kit to be used by the resistance groups. These included cheaply made pistols and other weapons that could be dropped in by air. Thousands of secret radios were hidden under floorboards, in cupboards, in large cookie tins or in suitcases (right). Sending and receiving messages right under the nose of the enemy, resistance radio operators were in constant danger of being captured, tortured, and executed, and many survived only weeks or months.

▼ Resistance groups used suitcase radios to transmit intelligence. Transmissions were kept as short as possible to stop the Germans pinpointing and capturing a radio operator.

▲ American Virginia Hall was an SOE agent in France who, despite her wooden leg, eluded capture by the German Gestapo for 15 months from 1941.

BEHIND ENEMY LINES

DURING WARTIME, THERE IS NO MORE DANGEROUS PLACE FOR A SPY TO BE THAN BEHIND ENEMY LINES. GETTING IN AND OUT SAFELY AND SECRETLY WERE PRIORITIES. ANYONE CAUGHT AS A SPY USUALLY FACED INTERROGATION AND SOMETIMES TORTURE AND DEATH.

All of the countries sent agents behind enemy lines to spy on military activity, to work with resistance groups, or to carry out sabotage. In 1944, for instance, two U-boats landed eight German agents, four on a beach off Florida and four on Long Island in New York. Their mission was to sabotage factories and power stations throughout the USA, but they were betrayed to the FBI by one of their number, John Dasch.

LOOK CLOSER

The SOE built over 3,000 Welbikes – tiny folding motorcycles that fitted inside a small parachute drop container. Used by some agents out in the field, they were assembled in under 12 seconds.

In 1944, SOE agent William Stanley-Moss posed as a German policeman on the island of Crete.

He kidnapped a German general, Heinrich Kriepe, smuggling him to Egypt for interrogation.

◄ Members of a French Resistance unit are briefed before a mission. Many spies were sent behind enemy lines to work with, train, or organize resistance groups.

◄ *Many agents sent from Britain to work in occupied Europe were parachuted in secretly at night, or flown in using a Westland Lysander aircraft that only needed a small field on which to land or take off.*

VIOLETTE SZABO

Szabo (1921–45) was trained by the SOE and parachuted into German-held France in early 1944. She reorganized a Resistance unit on her first mission and later commanded units that sabotaged German transport links. She was captured and sent to Ravensbrück concentration camp, where she died in 1945. Virginia McKenna (above) played Szabo in the 1958 film *Carve Her Name with Pride.*

SABOTAGE

Spies sabotaged enemy factories, transport links, shipping and ammunition dumps. Many German supply trains through France were derailed by blowing up bridges, tunnels, or rail lines. Bombs were disguised as fake lumps of coal or hidden inside cans of vegetables. The Germans even created a chocolate bar grenade, discovered by British agents in Turkey.

THE REAL Q

THE INSPIRATION FOR Q FROM THE JAMES BOND MOVIES WAS AN ORDINARY BRITISH CIVIL SERVANT WHO, DURING WORLD WAR II, CREATED SOME OF THE MOST AMAZING GADGETRY.

Many ingenious spy gadgeteers worked on inventing devices throughout the war. Charles Fraser-Smith (1904–92) was one of the most resourceful of these people. He designed and organized the supply of realistic uniforms and other clothing as well as equipment that was used by Britain's MI6 and SOE spies, resistance workers, and escaping prisoners-of-war (POWs) deep inside occupied Europe.

Fraser-Smith used more than 300 different companies and organizations in and around London to manufacture his wares. Forged foreign banknotes were even printed in the basement of London's famous Science Museum.

CHARLES FRASER-SMITH Fraser-Smith (1904–1992) worked in Morocco before returning to Britain in 1940 to help with the war effort. He worked in the British Ministry of Supply (Clothing and Textile Department) and created hundreds of pieces of equipment. He bought a farm after the war and published his memoirs in the 1980s.

▲ Fraser-Smith hid banknotes, compasses, maps, and weapons in all kinds of items. Saws were fitted in shoelaces, knives in shoe soles (above), and film in shaving brushes.

SIMPLE GENIUS

With supplies of many items and materials scarce during wartime, Fraser-Smith conjured up ingenious solutions to difficult problems. When even small compasses sewn into clothes could be detected, he fitted magnetized needles inside matchsticks. The match could be dropped in a pond where it would point north, acting like a compass.

Fraser-Smith sabotaged Germany's U-boat life-jackets, which were manufactured in France.

He ordered the manufacturers to put itching powder into the vests worn under the jackets.

◀ When dampened, the top layer of these playing cards could be peeled back to reveal a map. Other maps were printed on handkerchiefs in invisible ink.

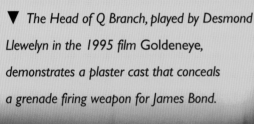

▼ The Head of Q Branch, played by Desmond Llewelyn in the 1995 film Goldeneye, demonstrates a plaster cast that conceals a grenade firing weapon for James Bond.

LOOK CLOSER

Fraser-Smith planned to make chocolate containing garlic so that British spies posing as Frenchmen or Spaniards in those countries would have realistic garlicky breath!

THE MAN WHO NEVER WAS

O NE OF THE MOST AMAZING AND SUCCESSFUL MISSIONS DURING WORLD WAR II WAS OPERATION MINCEMEAT. IT INVOLVED AN AGENT WHO WAS DEAD BEFORE THE MISSION STARTED.

The Italian island of Sicily had been identified by the Allies as the base for an invasion of southern Europe. What was needed was a major diversion to convince the Germans to place their forces elsewhere. British intelligence dressed up the dead body of a drowned man and built a cover story that he was Major William Martin, carrying important war plans in a locked briefcase chained to his body. The plans indicated an Allied invasion in Greece and the Balkans. The body was dropped off the coast of Spain. German spies found the body, photographed the documents, and alerted the German high command.

LOOK CLOSER

The cover story for "Major Martin" was that he had been flying to senior generals when his plane crashed in the Atlantic Ocean. His death was announced in The Times newspaper.

▼ Among the personal effects planted on Major Martin's body was a wallet containing theater ticket stubs, keys, identity tags, a watch, and the strap attaching the briefcase to his wrist.

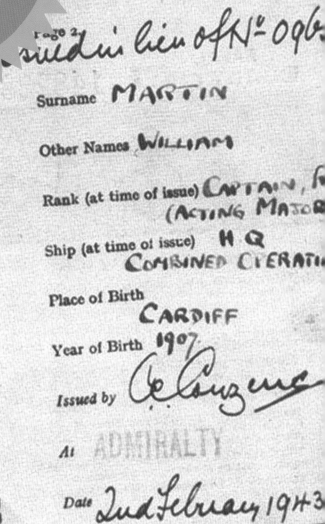

Surname MARTIN

Other Names WILLIAM

Rank (at time of issue) CAPTAIN, R (ACTING MAJOR

Ship (at time of issue) H Q COMBINED OPERATI

Place of Birth CARDIFF

Year of Birth 1907

Issued by

At ADMIRALTY

Date 2nd February 1943

In 1943, British prime minister Winston Churchill heard of Operation Mincemeat's success.

He received a telegram from his generals that read "Mincemeat Swallowed Whole"!

▼ Found on his body, this Naval Identity Card identified the invented William Martin as an acting major in British Combined Operations.

▲ The Germans moved the Italian fleet away from Sicily, and Operation Husky (above), the invasion of that island, took place in July 1943. The Germans and Italians were surprised by the attack and in just over a month, Sicily was captured and vital sea lanes in the Mediterranean secured.

Page 3.
Navy Form S.1511
NAVAL IDENTITY CARD No. 148228

Signature of Bearer
W. Martin

Visible distinguishing marks:
NIL.

SECRET IDENTITY

Secrecy was essential throughout Operation Mincemeat. The body was prepared in private, then sealed in a steel canister. It was carried aboard a submarine, Seraph, that sailed from Scotland in April, 1943. Even the submarine crew were not told about their mission. The canister was dropped into the sea just off the coast of Huelva in Spain, because the country was full of German spies. Huelva is where the dead man was buried (right). To this day, the real identity of the body remains a mystery.

WILLIAM MARTIN
BORN 29TH MARCH 1907
DIED 24TH APRIL 1943
BELOVED SON OF JOHN
GLYNDWYR MARTIN
AND THE LATE ANTONIA MARTIN OF
CARDIFF, WALES.
DULCE ET DECORUM EST PRO PATRIA MORI
R. I. P.

OTTO SKORZENY

OTTO SKORZENY (1908–1975) STARTED THE WAR AS A MEMBER OF HITLER'S BODYGUARD, AND THEN FOUGHT AS AN **SS** SOLDIER IN WESTERN AND EASTERN EUROPE.

Skorzeny was part of Operation Oak, which, in 1943, landed gliders high in the Apennine Mountains, and freed the captured Italian dictator, Benito Mussolini, who had been imprisoned by fellow fascists after the Allied invasion. Skorzeny was involved in other missions including a failed attempt to capture Yugoslavian resistance leader, Josip Tito. In Operation Greif in 1944, Skorzeny commanded a force of English-speaking German soldiers dressed in US army uniforms. They spread misinformation among Allied forces, cut telephone lines, and changed road signs, as well as sabotaging fuel dumps and blowing up bridges.

▲ *This is the mountaintop hotel, Campo Imperatore, where Mussolini was held prisoner until the daring rescue by the members of Operation Oak.*

LOOK CLOSER

As a young man Skorzeny had worked as an engineer but his daredevil streak saw him take part in over a dozen sword duels, one of which left him with a distinctive scar on his left cheek.

◄ *Italian dictator Benito Mussolini poses with the Germans who rescued him, including Skorzeny (left) who was promoted to major by Hitler for his part in the raid.*

◄ Skorzeny holds his name card during his trial in 1947 for war crimes. He was acquitted of the most serious charges and escaped from an internment camp in 1948.

HORTHY AND HITLER

Miklós Horthy, leader of Hungary (left), was one of Hitler's allies, but by late 1944 was wavering. It was thought he was about to surrender to the Russians, so Skorzeny kidnapped Horthy's son and forced Horthy to resign. A new pro-Hitler government was quickly installed.

THE MOST DANGEROUS MAN IN EUROPE

Dubbed the "most dangerous man in Europe," Skorzeny's spying and security activities continued after the conflict ended. He worked as a security advisor for governments in Spain, Egypt, and Argentina, where he was also Eva Peron's bodyguard. He was probably involved in the secret Odessa organization, obtaining false identities and helping to smuggle ex-SS officers to safety.

CODED SECRETS

With troops, spies, and missions all over the world, the amount of communication needed during World War II was vast. Various ingenious systems of keeping messages secret were employed by all sides.

The coding systems varied greatly. At their simplest, a person in charge of a safehouse might open or close the curtains to warn a spy of danger. At their most involved, people used complex code or cipher-making machines, or one-time pads – a cipher system used just once by an agent or their handler. Both sides broke some of the others' codes. The Germans broke the Black Code used by the US and, in 1941, were able to intercept and understand US messages from Cairo about enemy troops and tactics in North Africa. They passed these on to German generals on the ground.

◀ *Intelligence from the German Chiffrierabteilung (military cipher branch) enabled General Erwin Rommel (left) to win victories in North Africa in 1941.*

VELVALEE DICKINSON

American postal censors became suspicious of letters about dolls sent to addresses in Argentina. They were eventually traced by the FBI to a doll shop owner in New York, Velvalee Dickinson (1893–1980), who was spying on US navy ship movements for the Japanese. Dickinson used her own unique doll code. "A doll in a hula skirt" meant "a ship from Hawaii" and "doll hospital" meant "a damaged ship in for repair." Caught in 1944, Dickinson was sentenced to ten years in prison.

▲ A scene from the 2002 film, Windtalkers, shows a Navajo codetalker in action (left). Around 400 Navajo native Americans served in US forces in the Pacific and provided secret communications for the troops.

Messages were translated into Navajo and sent by radio to another Navajo codetalker.

The Navajo language is very complex and the Japanese were unable to break the code.

▶ A member of the French Resistance takes down a coded message using his radio. The Germans called these people *pianistes* and hunted them down ruthlessly.

STATION X

BLETCHLEY PARK WAS A RUNDOWN MANOR HOUSE NEAR LONDON THAT BECAME THE CENTER OF ALLIED ATTEMPTS TO BREAK GERMANY'S WARTIME CODES. ITS LOCATION WAS KEPT SECRET AND IT WAS CODENAMED STATION X.

The Germans used complex machines to create the Enigma and Lorenz codes. The Enigma machine was developed by Dr Arthur Scherbius in the early 1920s. An operator typed a message and then scrambled it by turning notched wheels called rotors. The code combinations grew into many millions as the Germans added more rotors and electronic circuits. Mathematicians in Poland made great progress shortly before World War II but it was an ongoing battle. The German Lorenz code was even more complex but the world's first programable electronic computer, Colossus, along with dedicated staff, made crucial breakthroughs.

▲ *This is one of more than 100,000 Enigma machines made by Germany. They scrambled messages into one of many billion secret codes.*

LOOK CLOSER

One breakthrough came in 1941 when the German trawler *Krebs* was captured off the coast of Norway. The trawler contained two Enigma machines along with code settings.

◀ *The 2001 movie Enigma highlighted the work done by the hundreds of scientists, thinkers, and mathematicians housed in the grounds of Bletchley Park.*

▲ Telephone engineer Tommy Flowers spent 11 months constructing the giant Colossus computer, which began work at Station X in 1943.

▲ The Bletchley Park mansion house was going to be demolished in 1938, but the head of MI6, Sir Hugh Sinclair, bought it with £7,500 of his own money.

CRACKED CODE

Cracking some of the Enigma and Lorenz codes turned the tide of battle in North Africa by letting Allied forces know where German supplies and forces were. It also meant that many secret communications from U-boats could be read, enabling the Allies to re-direct much of their shipping to avoid attacks. Many cargo ships were saved.

▼ A victim of a U-boat attack in 1941, HMS Barham (below) was the only active Allied battleship to be sunk by German submarines in World War II.

Paper tape instructions and data were fed into the Colossus computer by wheels at speeds of 31 mph.

Colossus read 5,000 characters per second. It cut the mathematical work needed from weeks to hours.

SPIES IN THE PACIFIC

THE WAR IN THE PACIFIC BEGAN IN DECEMBER 1941 WITH JAPAN'S SURPRISE BOMBING OF THE US PACIFIC FLEET MOORED AT PEARL HARBOR. THE GREAT DISTANCES BETWEEN LAND IN THE PACIFIC MEANT THAT CODED RADIO COMMUNICATIONS WERE VITAL.

Breaking Japanese radio codes was crucial to American success in the Pacific. The US knew Japan planned a massive attack in 1942, for example, but did not know where. When the JN-25b code was broken, the US knew that there would be an attack on a place codenamed AF. US troops on Midway island – an important refueling stop for long-distance planes – were told to send misleading radio signals that they were short of water. When Japanese messages were intercepted days later saying AF was short of water, the Americans knew the target was Midway. The resulting battle there was a major US victory.

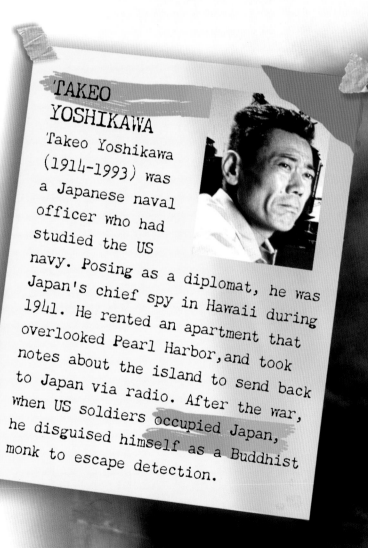

TAKEO YOSHIKAWA

Takeo Yoshikawa (1914-1993) was a Japanese naval officer who had studied the US navy. Posing as a diplomat, he was Japan's chief spy in Hawaii during 1941. He rented an apartment that overlooked Pearl Harbor, and took notes about the island to send back to Japan via radio. After the war, when US soldiers occupied Japan, he disguised himself as a Buddhist monk to escape detection.

PURPLE CODE MACHINE

The Japanese thought the code made by their Alphabetic Typewriter 97 (known as Purple in the USA) was unbreakable. In 1940, the US Army Signals Intelligence Service led by William Friedman broke the code, revealing Japanese plans in the Pacific. Japan's ambassador in Berlin, Baron Oshima, also used the code, so secrets about Germany were learned too.

Yoshikawa waited for the code words "east wind, rain" to be broadcast on his radio.

This signaled the Pearl Harbor attack, and he destroyed all of his spy kit and notes.

▼ A Japanese bomber wheels away after dropping its bombs on the US fleet at Pearl Harbor, sinking or damaging 21 ships and destroying 188 aircraft.

LOOK CLOSER

The mastermind behind the Pearl Harbor attack was Admiral Yamamoto. In April 1943, the US learned his secret route and sent fighter planes that shot down his aircraft.

Barbed wire, a deep trench, and barriers divide the German city of Berlin into east and west. This Berlin Wall, erected in 1961, became a powerful symbol of the Cold War. Attempts by people to cross to the other side, usually from east to west, often ended in death.

THE COLD WAR
Battle of the Superpowers

FROM THE END OF WORLD WAR II UNTIL THE START OF THE 1990S, THE SOVIET UNION AND THE UNITED STATES WERE LOCKED IN A COLD WAR, A FIERCE SPYING BATTLE FOR SUPREMACY.

SUPERPOWER SPYING

THE END OF WORLD WAR II SAW EUROPE IN TATTERS, GERMANY DIVIDED INTO TWO COUNTRIES, AND THE UNITED STATES AND SOVIET UNION AS THE DOMINANT NATIONS OR SUPERPOWERS.

Although the two never fought an open war, they were hostile and highly suspicious of each other. They engaged in an arms race and built up their intelligence agencies, including the Soviet Union's KGB and the US Central Intelligence Agency (CIA). Both countries formed alliances with friendly nations, dividing Europe into two power blocs with most of Western Europe allied to the United States, and Eastern Europe under Soviet control. Both sent hundreds of spies into enemy territory and neutral nations.

▼ *Air America appeared to be a civilian cargo and passenger airline, but it was run by the CIA. It was used to ferry anything from cattle and arms to spies and refugees in southeast Asia (below).*

MARCUS WOLF

A brilliant East German spymaster, Wolf (1923-2006) placed spies inside West Germany's government. These included Gunter Guillaume, who became an advisor to West German leader Willy Brandt. Wolf even recruited the head of West German counter-intelligence, Hans Joachin Tiedge. Wolf remained anonymous - the West did not have a photograph of him until 1978.

▲ This replica of the Great Seal hung in the US Ambassador's office in Moscow. It contained an ingenious KGB listening device that remained undetected for nearly eight years.

LOOK CLOSER

The Great Seal bug had no power supply, which made it hard to detect. To activate it, **KGB** agents would beam a radio signal to it from a van parked outside.

STASI SPIES

East Germany was a staunch ally of the Soviet Union. Its Ministry for State Security, the Stasi, was one of the most powerful of all the Cold War spying organizations. The Stasi employed hundreds of thousands of spies and informers inside East Germany, some equipped with secret buttonhole cameras (above). Stasi agents also secretly filmed homes and offices.

A NEST OF SPIES

AFTER WORLD WAR II, THE ALLIED POWERS DIVIDED THE FORMER GERMAN CAPITAL OF BERLIN INTO FOUR ZONES. THE WHOLE CITY WAS IN SOVIET-CONTROLLED EAST GERMANY.

As the Cold War developed, Berlin became a nest of spies, with agents and double agents on both sides. Gathering information from the enemy and passing false information to the enemy were the key weapons as each side tried to gain the upper hand. The main operators were the Soviet KGB and the American CIA, followed closely by Britain's MI6 and the East German Stasi. There were also up to 80 other secret service agencies with spies working in the city.

A DIVIDED CITY

The US, Britain, France, and the Soviet Union divided Berlin between them. The Soviets controlled the eastern side, while the others ran the western sectors.

1 Checkpoint Charlie
2 Brandenburg Gate
3 Stasi HQ
4 KGB HQ
☐ East Germany

▼ *The original 18th-century Brandenburg Gate was destroyed in World War II, and a copy built in the 1950s. It stood in the no-man's land between East and West Berlin.*

LOOK CLOSER

Around 5,000 Germans managed to escape across the Berlin Wall to West Berlin, and so to the west. Another 5,000 were caught, and 191 were killed attempting to cross.

THE BERLIN WALL

On 13 August 1961, Berliners awoke to find their city divided by a barrier of barbed wire fences. The East German government built the barricade to stop East Germans escaping to West Germany. Later, the fence was replaced with a concrete wall. The wall remained in place until 9 November 1989, a terrifying symbol of the divided city and country.

▶ *Checkpoint Charlie was one of the closely guarded crossing-points between East and West Berlin.*

THE BERLIN TUNNEL

One of the most daring of the Cold War intelligence operations in Berlin took place in 1954. The CIA and MI6 started to dig a 1,476-foot tunnel underneath the telephone lines used by the Soviet military HQ in Berlin. The plan was to listen in on Soviet messages. They hoped to get an early warning of any planned Soviet invasion of the West. Years later, the Western intelligence agencies discovered that the Soviets knew all about the tunnel. They had been tipped off by the British double-agent George Blake.

▶ *Armed police guard part of the Berlin Tunnel, which was discovered on 22 April 1956.*

The KGB had intelligence about the plan to build the Berlin Tunnel right from the start.

They decided to let the tunnel go ahead and to use it to pass false information to the West!

THE CAMBRIDGE SPIES

A NUMBER OF WELL-CONNECTED, SMART YOUNG MEN, ALL STUDENTS AT ENGLAND'S CAMBRIDGE UNIVERSITY, WERE RECRUITED IN THE 1930S TO SPY FOR THE SOVIET UNION. THESE SPIES BECAME IMPORTANT FIGURES IN BRITISH GOVERNMENT OR SPYING ORGANIZATIONS.

During and after World War II, the Cambridge spies had access to thousands of critical secrets about atomic bombs, weaponry, undercover missions, and the identity of British spies. When three of them, Maclean, Burgess, and Philby, worked in the United States after the war, they also passed on American secrets. The damage done would have been greater if the Soviets had been less suspicious.

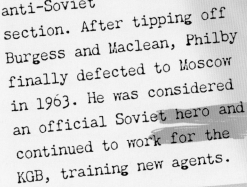

KIM PHILBY
Harold "Kim" Philby (1912-1988) worked in MI6 and in 1944, he was promoted to lead their anti-Soviet section. After tipping off Burgess and Maclean, Philby finally defected to Moscow in 1963. He was considered an official Soviet hero and continued to work for the KGB, training new agents.

LOOK CLOSER

Soviet spy Konstantin Volkov threatened to defect in 1945 and name 250 KGB spies working in Britain. Philby tipped off the Soviet Union. They captured Volkov in Turkey and executed him.

◄ These pictures show four of the Cambridge spies clockwise from top left: Anthony Blunt, Donald Maclean, Guy Burgess, and Kim Philby.

▲ *The Wren Library, part of Trinity College in Cambridge where Philby, Maclean, Burgess, and Blunt studied, becoming sympathetic to communism and, eventually, Soviet spies.*

In 1949, decoded Soviet messages showed that spies in Britain leaked wartime secrets.

Philby was asked to track down a Soviet spy codenamed Homer. He knew it was Donald Maclean.

Maclean and Burgess vanished in 1951. They surfaced in Moscow five years later.

THE FOURTH MAN

Rumors of a fourth member of the spy ring were rife, yet despite being questioned 11 times, Anthony Blunt led a respectable life. He was appointed Surveyor of the King's Pictures in 1945 and continued under Queen Elizabeth II. He finally admitted to being a Soviet spy in 1964, but this fact was only made public in 1979.

◄ *Blunt looked after the thousands of paintings and drawings owned by the British royal family and was knighted in 1956.*

FRIEND OR FOE?

As the Cold War progressed, both sides tried to protect their own interests at home and influence affairs abroad. The methods used were often secretive, shady, and sometimes even illegal.

Spies and spy agencies were involved in supporting friendly foreign governments or overthrowing unfriendly ones, often by funding and training rebel groups. The CIA, for example, engineered the removal of Chile's elected leader, Salvador Allende, in 1973. Meanwhile, the KGB trained and supported members of the MPLA forces during the Angolan Civil War in the 1970s. The KGB also helped the left-wing Sandinista movement, which ran Nicaragua from 1979 to 1990.

THE COINTELPRO PROGRAMME

From 1956 to 1971, COINTELPRO, the US Counter-Intelligence Programme, was directed by the FBI chief, J. Edgar Hoover (1895–1972), seen here seated at his desk. COINTELPRO investigated and discredited many people inside the United States, from left-wing political groups to civil rights workers. FBI agents planted bugs and infiltrated groups, carrying out more than 200 black bag operations (secret break-ins and burglaries).

▼ Contra rebels fighting Nicaragua's Sandinista government receive American training. The CIA funded the Contras as well as supplying the Freedom Fighter's Manual, a sabotage booklet.

► Afghan rebels ride on the way to an attack on Soviet troop positions in 1980. A KGB agent, Mitalin Talybov, attempted to poison Hafizullah Amin, the leader of Afghanistan in 1979.

LOOK CLOSER

The CIA leader of Operation Ajax, James Lockridge, slipped into Tehran, Iran, in 1953. His real name was Kermit Roosevelt, and he was the grandson of President Theodore Roosevelt.

OPERATION AJAX

Fears of a communist takeover in Iran, a major supplier of oil to the West, caused MI6 and the CIA to organize a coup in 1953 to topple Mohammad Mosaddeq, Iran's prime minister. Mosaddeq (above) had been elected fairly and was popular with many ordinary Iranians. But he was removed from power and held under house arrest until his death 14 years later.

SPYING IN THE MIDDLE EAST

THE MIDDLE EAST HAS BEEN AN ACTIVE REGION FOR SPYING, ESPECIALLY SINCE THE FORMATION OF ISRAEL AS A COUNTRY FOR JEWISH PEOPLES IN 1948. ISRAEL BUILT STRONG SPYING AGENCIES SUCH AS THE MOSSAD AND IS FREQUENTLY IN CONFLICT WITH NEIGHBORING ARAB NATIONS AS WELL AS THE PALESTINIANS, WHO HAD PREVIOUSLY OCCUPIED THE LAND.

Many Arab nations have attempted to place spies inside Israel. Egypt's Raafat Al-Haggan, posing as Jack Beton, was one of the most successful. He worked inside Israel for 17 years before leaving in 1973 with detailed maps of Israel's Bar Lev fortifications. Israel has also managed to place a number of their key Mossad agents inside neighboring Arab countries.

In the 1960s, Israel paid France for 50 Mirage fighters which they did not receive.

So they paid engineer Alfred Frauenknecht US $200,000 to copy thousands of Mirage blueprints.

▶ Israeli forces perform military maneuvers on the 40th anniversary of the 1967 Six Day War during which Israel captured important territory from Syria and Egypt.

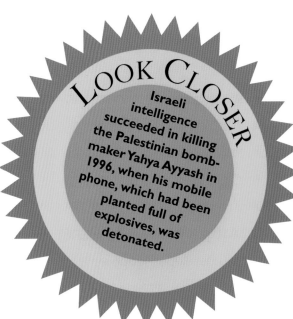

LOOK CLOSER

Israeli intelligence succeeded in killing the Palestinian bomb-maker Yahya Ayyash in 1996, when his mobile phone, which had been planted full of explosives, was detonated.

▲ *Egyptian soldiers capture the Bar Lev line of fortications during the 1973 Yom Kippur War when much of the Sinai Peninsula was re-taken from Israel, in part due to intelligence supplied by Egyptian spy Raafat Al-Haggan.*

THE MOSSAD

This Israeli intelligence agency was formed on 13 December, 1949 as a central organization to coordinate existing security services. Over the years, Mossad missions have included stealing many military secrets and the assassination of a number of terrorist leaders, as well as hunting down the Nazi war criminal, Adolf Eichmann, in Argentina, and those responsible for killing Israeli athletes in Germany at the 1972 Olympics.

ELI COHEN

In 1960, Eli Cohen (1924–1965) was recruited by the Mossad to spy in Syria. Posing as a businessman who held lavish parties, Cohen worked his way into the upper echelons of the ruling Baath Party and was given tours of military fortifications. Caught in 1965, he was tried (left below) and hanged. The intelligence he had sent helped the Israelis to capture the Golan Heights during the 1967 Six Day War.

SPIES IN THE SKY

SPYING IN THE COLD WAR LITERALLY TOOK OFF AS SATELLITES AND SPY PLANES HIGH ABOVE THE EARTH SENT BACK INTELLIGENCE OF RIVAL NATIONS' NUCLEAR POWER STATIONS, MISSILE BASES, AND OTHER SECRET FACILITIES.

Both sides developed jet-powered spy planes that traveled fast or at high altitude to avoid detection. One Soviet aircraft, the ML-17 *Mystic* was developed to have two roles – as a high-altitude spy plane and also as a US spy balloon killer (see page 105).

Incidents such as the capture of Gary Powers saw both sides turn more and more to spy satellites. These orbit high above Earth out of the range of missiles and enemy interceptor aircraft. The first models such as the Soviet *Zenit* satellites took high-resolution photos of parts of the Earth's surface. Later satellites were able to intercept communication signals and send them back to ground stations for decoding.

▲ *The U-2 spy plane was specially designed to help the US gather information about the Soviet missile program.*

In May 1960, a U-2 spy plane piloted by Gary Powers was shot down over the Soviet Union.

The US issued a cover story to the media, stating that a weather plane had flown off course over Turkey.

The US were very embarrassed when the Soviets exhibited the pilot and parts of the spy plane.

CAUGHT!

Gary Powers (1929-77) was an experienced jet pilot recruited by the CIA. When he was shot down over the Soviet Union, Powers did not use the poison pin hidden in a hollowed-out coin to commit suicide. He was sentenced to ten years in prison but after two years was exchanged for Rudolf Abel, the Soviet who had stolen US atomic secrets.

EAST VERSUS WEST

The earliest Soviet spy satellites called Zenit carried out over 500 missions from 1961 until 1994. Corona was the codename given to the first series of US spy satellites, which carried out more than 140 missions from 1960. Early Corona satellites carried 31,500 feet of film. Once a strip of film had been used, it was ejected from the satellite in a "bucket." This floated down under a parachute until caught by an aircraft.

LOOK CLOSER

Getting the images back from the early spy satellites could be a slow process. The photos taken by US satellites of the start of the 1967 Six Days War did not arrive until the war had ended!

▼ This image of the Pentagon – headquarters of the US Department of Defense – was taken from space by an early Corona spy satellite.

SPY BALLOONS

Before they had satellites or the U-2, the Americans twice used balloons fitted with advanced cameras to spy deep inside Soviet territory. In 1956, 448 balloons were released from Scotland, Germany, Turkey, and Norway and drifted over the Soviet Union. More than 300 were shot down and only 44 camera pods were recovered. The second attempt the following year featured a handful of high-tech balloons released in the Pacific that floated westwards over the Soviet Union. They almost got there, but were captured in Poland.

ON THE BRINK

IN OCTOBER 1962, TENSIONS BETWEEN THE TWO SUPERPOWERS BECAME SO GREAT THAT THE WORLD FEARED IT WAS ON THE BRINK OF AN ALL-OUT NUCLEAR WAR. SUDDENLY, ALL EYES WERE ON THE SMALL CARIBBEAN ISLAND OF CUBA.

Cuba was just 90 miles off the coast of the US mainland. Full of American-run sugar plantations and other businesses, they were seized by the Cuban government shortly after Fidel Castro came to power in 1959. He aligned himself with the Soviet Union and its allies. In the middle of 1962, Soviet ships began ferrying materials to construct bases on the island capable of launching nuclear missiles. When these were discovered by spies, there was uproar.

October 1962 saw the two sides exchange threats and US president Kennedy order a naval blockade of the island, to prevent the arrival of further Soviet ships. The Cuban missile crisis ended on 28 October when the Soviets agreed to remove the bases and missiles. In return, the US agreed not to invade Cuba.

> The spy Colonel Oleg Penkovsky handed over secret Soviet missile plans to the CIA.

> The plans allowed the USA to identify the Soviet missile bases on Cuba.

▶ A battery of Soviet SA-75 Dvina ground-to-air missiles lie in wait for enemy aircraft.

Americans crowd around television sets in a shopping center as President Kennedy delivers a speech on the Cuban missile crisis. Some Americans feared a catastrophic war.

MISSILE BASES

Spies on the ground and U2 spyplane missions in October 1962 revealed the construction of missile bases like the one below at Mariel Naval Port on Cuba. The Soviet SS-4 and SS-5 nuclear missiles to be housed there would have a potential range of 2,500 miles, bringing major US cities such as New York, Chicago, and Washington well within range for the first time.

LAUNCH STANDS

17 MISSILE ERECTORS

CASTRO

Fidel Castro (1926–) was a trained lawyer who became Cuba's leader in 1959. In 1961, a group of CIA-trained Cuban rebels landed at the Bay of Pigs to remove him from power. This was one of a number of unsuccessful CIA attempts to kill or unseat the fiery Cuban leader. Castro ruled Cuba until 2008.

DEATH TO SPIES

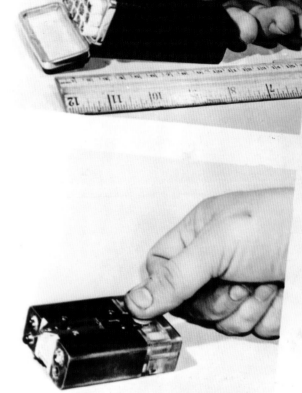

S PIES AND DEFECTORS OPERATED DURING THE COLD WAR WITH THE THREAT OF DEATH AROUND EVERY CORNER. THE SOVIET RED ARMY HAD A SPECIAL DEPARTMENT KNOWN AS SMERSH, WHICH MEANS "DEATH TO SPIES."

Dissidents (people critical of a government), spies who switched sides, and leaders of hostile countries were all targets for assassins during the Cold War. The United States attempted to assassinate Fidel Castro on many occasions. The Soviet Union and its allies tried to silence a number of critics and former spies by assassinating them. One assassin for the KGB, Bogdan Stashinsky, defected to the West in 1961. He admitted killing two Russian dissidents, Lev Rebet and Stefan Bandera, by using a poison gas spray hidden in a rolled-up newspaper.

▼ *This ordinary-looking lipstick converts into a single-shot pistol and was issued to an unknown KGB agent in 1965. The KGB nicknamed this weapon "the kiss of death."*

▲ *In April 1954, Nikolai Khokhlov (right) has a meeting in Frankfurt with the man he was supposed to assassinate, Georgi Okolovich.*

KGB agent Nikolai Khokhlov was sent to kill Georgi Okolovich, a Russian living in West Germany.

Khokhlov warned Okolovich and became a target himself, surviving a KGB assassination attempt.

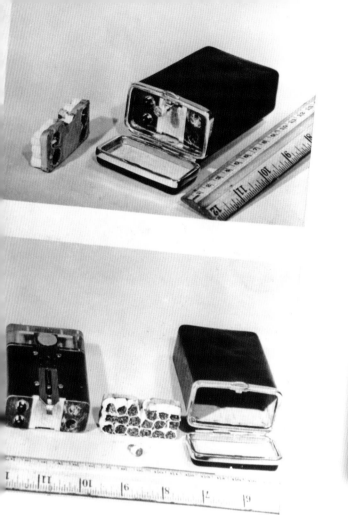

GEORGI MARKOV

Markov (1929-1978) defected from Bulgaria to the West in 1969. He worked as a writer, making radio broadcasts criticizing the Bulgarian government. He posed a threat to the government because his views were popular with the people in Bulgaria, so assassins were sent to kill him. In 1978, he was walking across Waterloo Bridge in London when a stranger jabbed him with his umbrella. Markov died three days later.

▲ These are photographs of the cigarette case weapon carried by assassin Nikolai Khokhlov. The case housed a gun hidden behind the fake tops of cigarettes that could fire poison pellets or steel bullets.

LOOK CLOSER
The Chamber was the nickname for KGB laboratory No.12 in Moscow that produced many secret weapons including poison pen sprays and bombs, and guns hidden in bags and briefcases.

RICIN PELLET

Markov's death was a mystery until a tiny pellet (above) was discovered in his leg. This pellet was drilled with holes that had contained the deadly poison ricin. This had been fired into Markov's leg from the umbrella tip. The assassin remains unknown, but it had not been the first attempt on Markov's life. Bulgarian agents had previously tried to poison his food.

YEAR OF THE SPY

A THAWING IN THE HOSTILE RELATIONS BETWEEN THE UNITED STATES AND THE SOVIET UNION WAS UNDERWAY BY 1985, BUT THAT DID NOT STOP THE SPYING. IN FACT, WITH THE REVELATION OF AGENTS' ACTIVITIES, 1985 IS REMEMBERED AS THE "YEAR OF THE SPY."

After providing valuable information for nearly 20 years, the most productive Soviet spy in Britain, Oleg Gordievsky, defected in 1985. Partly as a result, both Britain and the Soviets would expel around 25 diplomats suspected of being spies. In the United States, a whole host of spies were found not only working for the Soviet Union but also for China and, in the case of Jonathan Pollard, Israel. Pollard supplied Israel with details of missiles and other weapons before his arrest.

JOHN WALKER
Former US Navy warrant officer, John Walker (b.1937) seemed to be a loyal American who was strongly against communism. In reality, Walker had been spying for Soviet intelligence since 1967. He recruited his brother Arthur and his son Michael to obtain secrets as well. The spy ring was uncovered in 1985. John Walker is still in prison.

◀ A Tomahawk missile is fired from the cruiser, USS Shiloh. Walker supplied the Soviets with secrets about the missile's range, abilities, and weaknesses.

Oleg Gordievsky, a KGB agent, was actually a double agent who was working for the British.

Suspected by his Soviet handlers in 1985, he suddenly boarded a train from Moscow to Finland.

Contacting British intelligence, he was smuggled into Finland and then on to the UK.

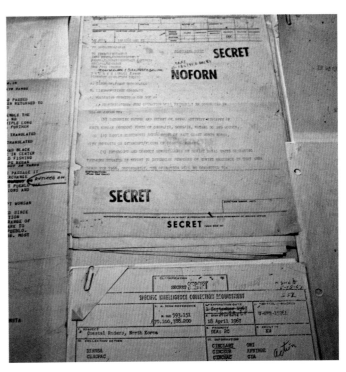

▲ Using information from the Walker spy ring, the US spyship, USS Pueblo, along with its secret documents (above), was captured by North Korean forces in 1968 and never returned.

LOOK CLOSER

Larry Wu-Tai Chin sent so much secret information to Chinese intelligence that each batch would take a team of translators at least two months to translate into Mandarin.

LARRY WU-TAI CHIN

After serving as a Chinese translator in the US Army during the Korean War, Larry Wu-Tai Chin (1918–86) joined the CIA in 1952. He began feeding sensitive information back to Chinese intelligence. Chin spied for China for over 30 years until his arrest in 1985.

► Larry Wu-Tai Chin on the way to court in 1985. He was paid hundreds of thousands of US dollars by China for his spying.

Security staff work in front of a giant bank of surveillance screens carrying high-resolution footage of a city taken with CCTV cameras. Despite round the clock surveillance of some locations, spies are still often needed to investigate an area in detail.

Communications House Cam 2
Eng 272

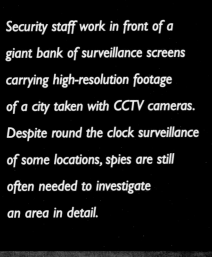

00 Br. WEST

0410288

TREASURY BUILDING -
PARLIAMENT SQ

SPYING IN THE 21ST CENTURY

Stealth and Electronics

tory House Eng Eng 231

t THOMAS HOSP. — WEST ROOF

WHEN THE COLD WAR ENDED AT THE START OF THE 1990S, SUPERPOWER SPYING DID NOT. NEW THREATS AND RISKS TO SECURITY HAVE GROWN AND SPIES ARE LEARNING TO COMBAT THEM.

NEW THREATS

ORGANIZED CRIME, LARGE-SCALE DRUGS DEALING, AND WARS IN OTHER COUNTRIES HAVE ALL BECOME TARGETS FOR 21ST-CENTURY SPYING. BUT THE GREATEST THREAT TO MANY NATIONS' SECURITY IS NOW FROM TERRORIST ATTACKS.

The most infamous terrorist group today is al-Qaeda. It seeks to rid all Muslim countries of western influence and has attacked targets worldwide. Spy agencies track down terrorists by tracing emails, mobile phone calls, and money transfers, as well as aerial spying for terrorist camps and infiltrating terrorist cells.

▲ A thermal imager fitted to the dashboard of a car allows agents to spot people and vehicles even in total darkness by sensing the infrared energy emitted from living things and warm vehicle engines.

Four airliners were hijacked over the United States on 11 September 2001 by al-Qaeda terrorists.

Two were flown into the World Trade Center and one into the Pentagon in Washington; one crashed in a field.

SPY ROBOTS

Unmanned Aerial Vehicles (UAVs) are robotic aircraft developed to fly undetected through danger areas. They take photographs, or monitor terrorist or criminal targets. In 2005, an MQ-1 Predator UAV (above), controlled by the CIA and fitted with a Hellfire missile, killed al-Qaeda explosives expert Haitham al-Yemeni in Pakistan.

◄ The second hijacked airliner flies toward the twin towers of New York's World Trade Center. The 9/11 attacks caused more than 2,700 deaths, shocked the world, and saw a massive increase in spying on terrorist groups.

CHINA SPIES

CHINA'S INTELLIGENCE NETWORK IS SHROUDED IN SECRECY BUT ONE THING IS CERTAIN – CHINESE SPIES ARE AT WORK IN MANY MAJOR COUNTRIES ALL AROUND THE WORLD.

Over decades, Chinese spies have built up large networks of contacts in Europe, Australia, and the United States. Chinese spies are rarely placed high up in other countries' spy services. They usually supply analysts with small amounts of information that can be pieced together. These include secrets such as the workings of industrial computer software, military secrets about the W88 nuclear warhead, night vision technology, and the engine used to power the F16 jet fighter.

▼ These offices are the local headquarters of China's Ministry of State Security (MSS) in Wuhan. The MSS is responsible for much of China's spying abroad.

LOOK CLOSER

In 2001, the FBI arrested Fei Ye and Ming Zhong as they were boarding a plane for China. Their suitcases contained blueprints of computer microchips and 8,800 pages of technical data.

In 2004, Chinese agent Moo Ko-Suen tried to buy a *Black Hawk* engine to ship back to China.

The Chinese wanted to pull the engine apart, to produce copies for their own helicopters.

▲ *Three American UH-60 Black Hawk helicopters hover in the air. Chinese spies have attempted on several occasions to buy the helicopter's engines and other advanced systems.*

CHI MAK

Chi Mak became a US citizen in 1985, working as an electrical engineer for a defense company. He copied documents about military equipment and sent them to China. He was arrested in 2005, as were his brother and sister-in-law. Chi Mak was sentenced to 24 years in prison.

CHEN YONGLIN

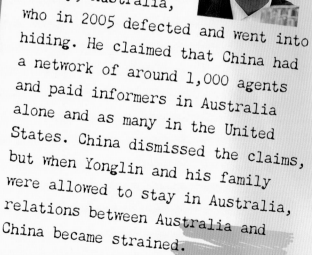

Chen Yonglin was a junior Chinese diplomat working in Sydney, Australia, who in 2005 defected and went into hiding. He claimed that China had a network of around 1,000 agents and paid informers in Australia alone and as many in the United States. China dismissed the claims, but when Yonglin and his family were allowed to stay in Australia, relations between Australia and China became strained.

CYBERSPIES

Less than 30 years ago, there was no Internet. The dramatic rise in computer use has created opportunities both for cyberspies to obtain secrets and for agents trying to counter and catch spies.

Agencies use computers to search records and databases, as well as break codes, and monitor emails, and other communications. But with valuable information held, not on paper, but as electronic data, computers pose a major threat. Skilled spies can hack into military or government computers to disrupt them or steal data. They sometimes use remote access tools to gain control of a computer from another location or keyboard loggers that record everything typed on a keyboard. This makes possible the theft of passwords, emails, and other information.

▲ These radomes at Menwith Hill, England, are believed to be part of the top-secret Echelon project – a network of bases run to intercept satellite communications.

▲ Powerful computer technology enabled the American Ikonos spy satellite to take this image of a suspected Iraqi nuclear weapon facility in 2003.

COMPUTER SECURITY

Protecting a country's computer networks is a major part of counter-intelligence work. Since 2003, there have been a series of attacks on government and military computers in the US, nicknamed Titan Rain. Skilled spies can disguise their identity making it hard to know if attacks are just curious individuals exploiting a gap in security or an organized attempt at spying by a group or another nation.

COMPUTING ON THE MOVE

Power-packed computer technology has now been shrunk so small that it can easily be carried by spies. It comes in the form of smartphones, laptops, or PDAs (Personal Digital Assistants) out in the field. It can easily be used to gain information, search databases, and infiltrate computer networks while the agent is on the move. However, agents have to be careful to prevent their hardware and its data falling into enemy hands. One 2007 report indicated that FBI agents had lost or had stolen 160 laptops in under four years!

▲ *This wearable computer can project a computer screen image directly onto the eye of the user.*

▼ *A staff member working for a security agency monitors computer traffic across networks of linked computers at a secret computer network center – location unknown.*

LOOK CLOSER

In 2006, the UK's MI6 stopped a major operation in Colombia when one of their spies lost their USB memory stick. In 2008, the agency began to recruit spies using the website Facebook!

THE FUTURE OF SPYING

SPYING IS NOT GOING TO STOP — WHEREVER THERE ARE VITAL SECRETS AND PEOPLE'S SECURITY AND PROSPERITY DEPEND ON THEM, THERE WILL BE SPIES TRYING TO FIND OUT THE DETAILS. *HOW* COUNTRIES SPY, THOUGH, IS EXPECTED TO ALTER IN THE FUTURE.

Human agents are large, and sometimes easily spotted and caught. If captured, they may reveal details of other missions under questioning or torture, or be turned to spy against their own country. Machines can have their data erased or be primed to self-destruct, so are likely to be used in spying more and more. Nanotechnology is the science of constructing microscopic machines. Future nanobots may be sprinkled like smart dust over electronic devices and rooms where they could work together to survey and report back all that they sense.

LOOK CLOSER

Shrinking technology may be able to improve human hearing or sight, or give people the ability to communicate wirelessly through chips implanted in their bodies.

▼ *A future nanobot, shaped like a crab, scuttles across an electronic circuit board. It might be sabotaging the device or tapping into the device's electronic signals and recording them.*

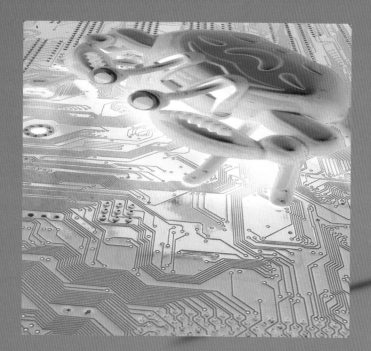

▶ *This dragonfly micro aerial vehicle (MAV) is tiny and weighs less than a quarter of a gram. Future MAVs may be able to hover or fly unnoticed, spying on people or photographing documents.*

In 1999, scientists in New York hid an experimental short message in a strand of human DNA.

The scientists' secret message echoed the 1944 D-Day landings: "June 6 invasion: Normandy."

▶ Future secret messages may be made almost impossible to detect or break by encoding them in the DNA of living things – the molecules in a cell that carry genetic information.

IDENTITY CHANGE

Human spies are still likely to be needed in some situations and the identity of important informers or defectors may need to be protected. In 2008, American Connie Culp, who had been badly disfigured by a shotgun, received a full face transplant. Future technologies may enable spies and defectors to change their identity with face and voice transplants at will.

▶ These Terminator androids are currently only found in sci-fi movies. However, future robots able to operate on land, sea, and in the air and space are expected to perform major intelligence-gathering missions.

SPY DOSSIERS

The names of many of the greatest spies have been lost to history and what we know about many others is at best sketchy. In some cases, key facts are still classified and remain secret. Much information is in the public domain, however, and what follows are brief profiles of 20 important spies and spymasters from all over the world.

CHANDRAGUPTA MAURYA (C.340 BCE-C.290 BCE), INDIAN
The founder of the Maurya Empire that spread throughout much of India, Maurya and his chief minister, Chanakya, made use of spying and assassination to build and extend the empire.

CHARLOTTE DE BEAUNE SEMBLANÇAY (1551-1617), FRENCH
This French noblewomen was recruited to spy on the French court by Catherine de Medici. As a member of Catherine's *Escadron Volant* (Flying Squadron) of beautiful female spies, Charlotte made friends with and seduced powerful noblemen to learn secrets.

WILLIAM WICKHAM (1761-1840), ENGLISH
A British politician, Wickham was sent to Switzerland as ambassador in 1795. From there, he established spy rings in France and Switzerland during the French Revolution (1789–1799) in an attempt to discredit the Revolutionaries and re-establish a monarch in France.

SARAH EDMONDS (1841-1898), CANADIAN
Wanting to fight for the Union during the American Civil War, Edmonds disguised herself as a man and joined the Union Army. She later spied on the Confederate forces by disguising herself as a black male slave and as an Irish laundry woman.

ÉTIENNE BAZERIES (1846-1931), FRENCH
Having fought as a soldier in Europe and Algeria, Bazeries developed a cipher cylinder with 20–30 discs which would later become the US Army M-94 device. In the 1890s, Bazeries broke a number of codes used by the French government, prompting them to employ him. Although he retired in 1899, he worked for France on ciphers during World War I.

SIDNEY REILLY (1873-1925)
Believed to have been born Georgi Rosenblum in Odessa, now the Ukraine, Reilly was given the nickname "Ace of Spies." He spied on forces during the Russo-Japanese War, on oilfields in Persia (Iran), and was smuggled into Germany during World War I to report back to British intelligence. Reilly lived a charmed life, but the master of deception was himself deceived, and lured back to Russia in the 1920s to take part in operations against the Bolshevik government. It was all a set-up and Reilly was captured and executed.

ORESTE PINTO (1889-1961), DUTCH
A brilliant counter-intelligence officer, Oreste was once called "the greatest living authority on security" by US president Dwight Eisenhower. During World War II, he worked with MI5 to root out potential threats to security and captured enemy spies and informers via intelligence and the questioning of arrivals to Britain.

SARAH AARONSOHN (1890-1917), PALESTINIAN
Born in Palestine, Aaronsohn was sickened by massacres by the Ottomans during World War I, and was part of the Nili ring of Jewish spies. She traveled throughout much of the Ottoman Empire, gathering intelligence secretly and passing it on to the British at their base in Egypt. Betrayed when one of her carrier pigeons was caught by the Ottomans, she was tortured for four days but committed suicide rather than give away any secrets.

WILLIAM FRIEDMAN (1891-1969), AMERICAN
Born in what is today Moldova, Friedman and his family moved to the United States where he became fascinated by codes and worked on them for the US War Department during World War I.

In World War II, he was head of the team that broke a number of Japanese codes, including the important Purple cipher. In 1952, he became chief cryptologist at the National Security Agency.

PRINCESS STEPHANIE VON HOHENLOHE (1891-1972), GERMAN

A member of the German aristocracy, Princess Stephanie was born in Austria and in the 1930s lived in London. Despite being a Jew, she knew Hitler and worked for German intelligence, supplying them with secrets gleaned from important figures in British and European business and politics.

SIDNEY COTTON (1894-1969), AUSTRALIAN

An Australian inventor, businessman, and pilot, Cotton flew missions in World War I in the Royal Naval Air Service. A pioneer of high-altitude aerial spying, he was contacted by French intelligence and MI5 in the 1930s, and made numerous flights for them over Italy, North Africa, and Germany. Given command of the RAF's first aerial spying squadron during World War II, he spied, ferried arms, and carried out sabotage operations.

ALFRED FRENZEL (1899-1968), CZECHOSLOVAKIAN

Codenamed Anna, Frenzel was a West German MP blackmailed by Czech spies about his past as a member of the Czech Communist Party. Frenzel passed on many West German government documents to his Czech handlers. He was caught in 1960 but was allowed to leave Germany in a spy swap in 1966.

MOE BERG (1902-1972), AMERICAN

A famous Major League baseball player, Berg had first spied on the harbor and

streets of Tokyo in 1934, using a movie camera hidden under his coat. He joined the OSS in 1943 and was parachuted into Yugoslavia to check on resistance forces, spied on German nuclear power bases in Norway, and on German atomic bomb makers throughout occupied Europe.

NANCY WAKE (1912-), NEW ZEALANDER

Living in Marseille, France, when World War II began, Wake started working as a courier for the French resistance and helped organize a large spy network. The Germans tried but failed to capture her as she crossed six times from France into Spain. Such was her success that, after the war, she was awarded medals by five countries (France, Britain, the USA, Australia, and South Africa).

DUSAN POPOV (1912-1981), YUGOSLAVIAN

Codenamed Tricycle during World War II, Popov was a talented double agent who worked for Germany but in actuality supplied the Allies with much valuable intelligence. He also helped in the plan to convince Germany that the D-Day landings were taking place at a different location to Normandy.

MOSHE MARZOUK (1926-1955), EGYPTIAN

An Egyptian Jew, Marzouk was recruited in the early 1950s to work as a spy for Israel. He was part of a group that carried out bombings in Egypt in 1954 but was captured and executed in 1955.

RYSZARD JERZY KUKLINSKI (1930-2004), POLISH

A colonel in the Polish Army, Kuklinski offered his services to the CIA. For the next decade, he passed some 30,000

pages of secret documents to the US, including the location of anti-aircraft bases in Poland and East Germany and how the Soviets hid secret locations from spy planes and satellites. The CIA ferried him out of Poland in 1981.

ROBERT HANSSEN (1944-), AMERICAN

Hanssen joined the FBI in 1976 and offered his services as a spy to the Soviet Union's military intelligence service, the GRU. He then gave up spying but in 1985 approached the KGB and until his capture in 2001, received over US$1.7 million in return for thousands of secrets including the identities of US spies. He is serving life imprisonment in the USA.

ODILE HARRINGTON (1961-), SOUTH AFRICAN

Harrington was recruited to work for South African intelligence. In 1986, she was sent to Zimbabwe to infiltrate the African National Congress (ANC). She posed as an anti-apartheid activist but one of her letters was opened by Zimbabwean intelligence and she was arrested and imprisoned in 1990.

ALEXANDER LITVINENKO (1962-2006), RUSSIAN

Recruited to work for the KGB in 1986, Litvinenko became a specialist in counter-terrorism and counter-intelligence. In 1998, he and other FSB staff accused their bosses of ordering assassinations. In 2000, he fled from Russia to London where he made further allegations. In November 2006, he suddenly fell ill and died. He had been poisoned by the radioactive substance polonium-210, but mystery surrounds whether this was an assassination by an intelligence agency.

GLOSSARY

■ **ABWEHR**
The spying and intelligence service for the German Armed Forces from 1921 to 1944.

■ **AGENT PROVOCATEUR**
A person, not always a spy, who is sent in to provoke others into performing rash and illegal actions.

■ **ASSASSIN**
A spy or person paid to plan and carry out the killing of someone considered a threat to national security.

■ **BLACK BAG JOB**
A slang name for a burglary or break-in to collect intelligence.

■ **BLACKMAIL**
To try to influence a person by unfair pressure or threats of revealing secrets about them.

■ **BUG**
A device that can record or transmit sound and send it to a receiver some distance away.

■ **CCTV**
A system of closed circuit TV cameras that monitors offices and public places, sending images to a security center.

■ **CHEKA**
The Russian secret police force that was founded in 1917 to serve the Communists led by Vladimir Lenin.

■ **CIA**
The Central Intelligence Agency of the United States, founded in 1947, and responsible for much of America's spying abroad.

■ **CIPHER**
A type of code (see below) in which each letter of the alphabet is represented by another letter, number, or symbol in a system.

■ **CODE**
The use of symbols, letters, or numbers to represent words and sentences to hide the real meaning of a secret message.

■ **COUNTER-INTELLIGENCE**
The part of spying devoted to stopping enemies from spying on a country that includes uncovering and capturing enemy spies.

■ **COURIER**
A spy who retrieves and delivers messages, documents, or other secret information.

■ **COVER STORY**
A false story about a person's identity and line of work used by a spy to complete their mission undetected.

■ **CYBERSPY**
A spy who works mainly using computers and other information technology.

■ **DEAD DROP**
A place used to hide packages, messages, or money for an agent or contact to collect.

■ **DEFECTOR**
A person, sometimes a spy, politician, or military figure, who ends their allegiance to their own country and seeks to live in another country.

■ **DGSE**
The French foreign intelligence service, formed in 1981.

■ **DIPLOMAT**
A person who works for a government and represents them in relations with other countries and governments.

■ **DOUBLE AGENT**
A spy who works for two intelligence services, spying *on* a country while pretending to spy *for* that country.

■ **FBI**
The Federal Bureau of Investigation, the United States' national police force that also investigates spying.

■ **FORGE**
To produce a seemingly identical yet fake copy of an object, often money or identity documents.

■ **GUERILLA**
Someone who belongs to a group that harasses and fights an enemy by ambushes and surprise hit-and-run attacks.

■ **INFILTRATE**
To secretly enter a group or rival intelligence organization to spy on it and report back.

■ **INTELLIGENCE**
Secret and potentially valuable information or news about an enemy or rival.

■ **KGB**
The *Komitet Gosudarstvenoy Bezopasnosti*, or Committee for State Security, which was the Soviet Union's secret service until the start of the 1990s.

■ **MI5**
The British domestic and foreign counter-intelligence service responsible for national internal security.

■ **MI6**
The British foreign intelligence service.

■ **MICRODOT**
A photographic reduction of a secret message so small it can be hidden in plain sight.

■ **MOLE**

A spy who manages to either work in or get close to another country's security service, sending intelligence back to a rival agency.

■ **MOSSAD, THE**

Israel's foreign intelligence agency, the Institute for Intelligence and Special Operations.

■ **OKHRANA**

A secret police force in Russia, formed in 1880 and active until 1917.

■ **OPERATIVE**

Another word for agent or spy in the service of an intelligence agency.

■ **OSS**

The Office of Strategic Services, an American intelligence agency formed during World War II.

■ **PROPAGANDA**

Spreading a particular message to try to influence public opinion or to make people perform certain actions.

■ **RECRUIT**

To obtain a new spy or member of an intelligence agency.

■ **SABOTAGE**

The destruction of, or interference with, an object that damages an enemy's production or transport.

■ **SAFEHOUSE**

A room or building that is not under surveillance or bugged by enemy agents which is used to store equipment, people or used as a base for meetings and missions.

■ **SMERSH**

A department of Russian intelligence, formed in 1943, that mainly worked at stopping and capturing enemy spies.

■ **SOE**

Short for the Special Operations Executive, this World War II organization was formed by the British to link with the Resistance and carry out spying and other missions in German-occupied Europe.

■ **SPYMASTER**

A person who controls or supervises the agents in a spy ring.

■ **SURVEILLANCE**

To closely watch one or more people or a place for a period of time.

■ **SVR**

Russia's foreign intelligence service, formed in 1991 shortly after the break-up of the Soviet Union and the KGB.

■ **TAPS**

Devices, also known as wiretaps and often used by spies, that allow telephone calls to be monitored and, sometimes, recorded.

FURTHER READING

SECRETS, LIES, GIZMOS AND SPIES
by Janet Wyman Coleman (International Spy Museum, 2006)

THE HISTORY OF ESPIONAGE
by Ernest Volkman (Carlton Books, 2007)

HIDDEN SECRETS
by David Owen (Firefly Books Ltd, 2002)

THE ENEMY WITHIN: A HISTORY OF SPIES, SPYMASTERS AND ESPIONAGE
by Terry Crowdy (Osprey Publishing, 2006)

WEBSITES

The website of the excellent International Spy Museum in Washington D.C. is full of features on spies and spying and details of how to visit:
http://www.spymuseum.org

A PBS website about the atomic spies of the 1940s with biographies and details:
http://www.pbs.org/wgbh/nova/venona/

Learn more about the Federal Bureau of Investigation (FBI) including past missions:
http://www.fbi.gov/aboutus.htm

A collection of informative profiles of leading spies:
http://www.spyschool.com/spybios/sbmenu.htm

Details of past missions and what MI5 does and does not do are available at this website:
http://www.mi5.gov.uk/output/history.html

Read Robert Baden-Powell's book, *My Adventures As A Spy* for free at this website:
http://www.pinetreeweb.com/bp-adventure01.htm

INDEX